DELHI DIALOGUE III

Delhi Dialogue III

BEYOND THE FIRST TWENTY YEARS OF INDIA-ASEAN ENGAGEMENT

Editors
S.T. DEVARE
VIBHANSHU SHEKHAR

ICWA

MANOHAR
2012

First published 2012

Some of the contents of this volume have been transcribed from the audio recordings. The text has been edited and suitably modified for the readers.

ISBN 978-81-7304-962-0

Published by

Ajay Kumar Jain *for*
Manohar Publishers & Distributors
4753/23 Ansari Road, Daryaganj
New Delhi 110 002

Typeset at

Digigrafics
New Delhi 110 049

Printed at

Salasar Imaging Systems
Delhi 110 035

Contents

About Delhi Dialogue

The Delhi Dialogue, an annual forum for India-ASEAN strategic dialogue, has come a long way in providing, perhaps, the most important avenue for debate and dialogue involving the policy makers, think tanks, academics and business leaders. The last three years of dialogue have generated a new momentum and urgency in not only broad-basing the debate over India-ASEAN relations, but also making it more innovative and outcome-driven. The Delhi Dialogue is hosted by the Ministry of External Affairs in partnership with the Indian Council of World Affairs (ICWA) and Federation of Indian Chambers of Commerce and Industry (FICCI), together with the support of the Institute of Southeast Asian Studies (ISEAS), SAEA Group Research and Economic Research Institute of ASEAN and East Asia (ERIA).

Three annual sessions of Delhi Dialogue have taken place. The Delhi-Dialogue I, organized by the FICCI and SAEA, and supported by India's Ministry of External Affairs and the ISEAS, was held on 21-22 January 2009. It was inaugurated by H.E. Shri Pranab Mukherjee, the then Minister for External Affairs, and H.E. Dr Surin Pitsuwan, ASEAN Secretary-General. The Delhi Dialogue II, held on 21-22 January 2010 saw the focus on regional security and cooperation with the theme of examining *India and Southeast Asia in the Changing Regional Economic Dynamics of Asia: Shared Interests and Concerns*. The Hon'ble External Affairs Minister of India, H.E. Shri S.M. Krishna and the Deputy ASEAN Secretary-General H.E. Mr Pushpanathan Sundram graced the Delhi Dialogue II.

The Delhi Dialogue III, held on 3-4 March 2011, was hosted by MEA in partnership with the Indian Council of World Affairs (ICWA) and FICCI, together with the support of ISEAS, SAEA Group Research and ERIA. The Delhi Dialogue III was focused on the central theme '*Beyond the First Twenty Years of India-ASEAN Engagement*' and developed a partnership platform for concerned stakeholder for coming together to build a safe, secure and prosperous region. Besides, the Delhi Dialogue III addressed five major themes—(a) Looking Towards 2012 and Beyond, (b) India-ASEAN Connectivity, (c) Nalanda as a Symbol of Asian Renaissance, (d) Enhancing India-ASEAN Cooperation in Critical Areas of Non-traditional Security Issues/Global Commons, and (e) India in the ADMM Plus and the EAS Process: The Next Decade. It sought to provide an additional avenue for policy makers, think tanks, academics and business leaders to engage in a manner that animates fresh policy thinking and innovative solutions to challenges facing the region.

WELCOME ADDRESSES

Shri Sudhir T. Devare

Shri Amit Mitra

Shri Sudhir T. Devare

Director General, Indian Council of World Affairs

Delhi Dialogue is a valuable opportunity for India with its deep commitment for close interaction and cooperation with our neighbours in Southeast Asia, to extend and expand our mutual understanding and trust. This third edition of the dialogue that began in 2009 and is titled *Beyond the First Twenty Years of India-ASEAN Engagement,* represents an ongoing and mutually beneficial foreign policy exercise between India and Southeast Asia, both at the high government level as well as at Track II. In this regard it is indeed a unique undertaking.

For the last two decades, India and ASEAN countries have steadily built their relationship both at bilateral as well as at multilateral level. Political exchanges including summits and economic cooperation have led to the development of a plan of action to implement the ASEAN-India partnership for peace, progress and shared prosperity for the years 2010-15, and a landmark agreement on India-ASEAN trade in goods.

> *"India believes that ASEAN is the core around which the process of economic integration in the Asia-Pacific and the emergence of an Asian Economic Community have revolved."*

India-ASEAN interaction began to take shape in the wake of the end of the cold war, the onset of globalization, the technological revolution in communication, and coincidentally with the initiation of economic reforms in India. The mutual desire for security, peace and prosperity in the Asia-Pacific region was the driving impulse for this process.

With India as well as ASEAN countries weathering the global financial crisis reasonably well, the two are today poised for an accelerated economic cooperation. India believes that ASEAN is the core around which the process of economic integration in the Asia-Pacific and the emergence of an Asian Economic Community have revolved. India on its part stands fully committed to realize this goal with its sustained economic growth of about 9 per cent per year.

India's engagement with Southeast Asia and East Asia is a key component of its foreign policy. India's interaction with the region generally known as Look East Policy has been a very positive development, which we all in India look upon with pride and satisfaction. India appreciates the support it has received over the years from ASEAN states for its membership in the ASEAN-centred fora such as the India-ASEAN Dialogue Partnership, the India-ASEAN Summit, the ASEAN Regional Forum (ARF), and the East Asia Summit (the EAS process). India has reaffirmed its commitment to the EAS.

“*The Delhi Dialogue aims at having an open and useful discussion on these and related important issues.*”

As we look to the years ahead, what should be the agenda for our cooperation in the political and security fields as well as in economic cooperation or multilateral engagement? A number of priority areas can be identified such as India-ASEAN connectivity, cooperation in the critical areas of non-traditional security issues or politico-security arrangements in the context of the EAS process, ARF, and the ADMM Plus. The Delhi Dialogue aims at having an open and useful discussion on these and related important issues.

India and Southeast Asia have enjoyed civilizational contacts. The project of the revival of the ancient Nalanda University with active support from countries in Southeast and East Asia is a testimony to our joint resolve to recreate our friendship and goodwill with roots in the past. India and Southeast Asia had intermingled and were intertwined with each other in ancient past to create a cultural amalgam. Rabindranath Tagore, a great poet and philosopher, whose 150th birth anniversary is being celebrated this year, had observed during his visit to Indonesia, "I see India everywhere, but I do not recognize it". The idea of a dialogue between India and ASEAN which commenced twenty years ago can hopefully produce a similar close bond and develop between us in modern times.

We trust that the statements of hon'ble Ministers and deliberation at the Delhi Dialogue will provide very useful and important inputs in charting a roadmap for our future shared destiny even as the two sides prepare for celebrating the commemorative summit of India and ASEAN in 2012.

Shri Amit Mitra

Secretary-General, Federation of Chambers of Commerce and Industry (FICCI)

Three years ago FICCI began this process of dialogue from Track II. What is fascinating is that from Track II we have a merger of Track II and Track I. The Secretary (East) Ms. Latha Reddy, Ministry of External Affairs, Government of India has been the moving force in the government taking the lead. We really appreciate that a seamless synthesis has developed. Mr. Ravindran of SAEA was there from the beginning and it was, to some degree, his idea from the Track II. Today we have grown in stature because of the synergy between Track I and Track II.

Two gauntlets have been thrown on the floor for us – (a) complete the services and investment end of the Comprehensive Economic Cooperation Agreement, and (b) reach the 70 billion dollar mark for the India-ASEAN trade. The ASEAN-India Business Council meeting, which began today, has, in fact, decided to focus precisely on these two themes The issue of food security and climate change are critical in our discourse in this dialogue.

We must acknowledge that the current Indian government has signed the Comprehensive Economic Cooperation Agreement with Japan, Comprehensive Economic Agreement with Korea, and, of course finally, the Free Trade Agreement with ASEAN, all looking in the direction of the East. So, it is not just a word to be said but it is something that we are hoping that the Indian government will now lead on to the inclusion of services and investment into the whole ASEAN space.

The gamut of India-ASEAN connectivity, such as trilateral highways, Mekong-India Economic Corridor, represents a complete architecture of the future, which is very fascinating indeed. Newly-married couples are going to Southeast Asia as honeymooners, creating wider popular constituencies within India. The ecosystem of ASEAN seems to be stamped in the genetic material of the next generation of India.

KEYNOTE ADDRESSES

H.E. Dr. Surin Pitsuwan

Shri S.M. Krishna

H.E. Pehin Dato' Lim Jock Seng

H.E. Mr. Kasit Piromya

H.E. Dr. Mari Elka Pangestu

H.E. Dr. Surin Pitsuwan

Secretary-General, ASEAN

The Third Delhi Dialogue comes at an opportune time as we have just finished one full year of ASEAN-India Free Trade Agreement in Goods. We have seen phenomenal growth in the exchange of our people, our officials, our academics, our media, and certainly our business people. Together we are 1.8 billion humanity, about three trillion combined GDP and a formidable force for the new centre of growth that is being recognized globally now – East Asia.

India and ASEAN are natural partners. Historically India traded, explored and sent cultural values, civilizations and religions to Southeast Asia and beyond. East Asia has become a new centre of growth, not because everybody else is in trouble but we ourselves have transformed the way in which we do business, the way in which we manage our cooperation and our affairs. East Asia has become a new market place of the world.

> *"The middle class of East Asia, the middle class of India and ASEAN could become that transmission belt of economic prosperity, of political transformation, of cooperation of new emerging architectures that we need to put in place in order to manage our new status as a new locomotive of growth of the global economy."*

When President Obama met with ten ASEAN leaders at the second summit in New York last September, he said, "For the US to get out of economic crisis we have to be able to export more, we have to be able to sell more." "When we look around who would be our market, who would be our consumers – you in East Asia, you in ASEAN."

Together, out of 1.8 billion, at least 300 million could be considered and classified as the middle class. The middle class of East Asia, the middle class of India and ASEAN could become that transmission belt of economic prosperity, of political transformation, of cooperation of new emerging architectures that we need to put in place in order to manage our new status as a new locomotive of growth of the global economy.

That is why we have put together an architecture of ASEAN Plus One, – and ASEAN Plus Three – with the East Asian economies of China, Japan, Korea, and ASEAN Plus Six – India, Australia, New Zealand, China, Japan, and South Korea. This new architecture is overarching, comprehensive and formidable both in terms of market, purchasing power, and in terms of the issues that we have to address together.

Henry Kissinger at the end of the last century observed that as far as the economic dynamism is concerned, as far as innovation is concerned, East Asia is equivalent to the twentieth-century Europe. But in terms of the process, mechanism and the institutions to address problems that could occur in East Asia, he said, the region is still the nineteenth-century Europe. In the past two or three decades, East Asia with ASEAN at the centre as fulcrum of new architectures of the region, as centrality of evolution in the region, has been playing that role or trying to come up with new effective political economic security architectures in East Asia responding to that riddle, to that observation that Mr. Henry Kissinger made at the end of the 1970s. This central role that ASEAN has been playing, this role of centrality, this fulcrum of emerging architectures as Mrs. Clinton put it, is more important now than ever because we are now the new centre of growth.

The focus is now on what is going on in East Asia – India, Southeast Asia, and the rest in East Asia. The region is now being examined, analysed, followed, and monitored more closely than ever before. When we failed before, for example, the economic crisis at the end of 1990s, we did not have negative impact on the global economy. But if something happens today to this new centre of growth, to this fulcrum of emerging architectures in East Asia, the impact is going to be far-reaching, globally felt and globally negative. That is why ASEAN and India's cooperation and relationship has assumed a new level of importance and urgency.

We need to go through all these issues of traditional security, non-traditional security, food security, energy security, climate change, pandemics, and natural disasters. All these are issues of fundamental importance to both sides and to the rest of East Asia and by extension, as mentioned earlier, to the rest of the global community.

Our task and mission today is to look back at what we have done in the past twenty years. Has our trade increased proportionately to our roles in the region, in the world? India is being recognized as 'I' in BRIC and pretty soon another 'I' Indonesia is going to get into that. ASEAN is being a permanent feature of the G20. Have we achieved the potential that we should be achieving in the past 20 years?

In the year 2007, our bilateral trade was above 50 billion. In 2008 we went into this crisis mode because of the world crisis and not because of our crisis. The year of 2009 was affected and we felt the impact of 2008. In 2010 we are beginning to climb back. The Indian Prime Minister Manmohan Singh had given us a charge and that charge is that by the year 2012 bilateral trade between India and ASEAN shall reach 70 billion US dollars. We can do it, but to achieve that, we need the contribution and participation of the private sector because they would be the nuts and bolts of any cooperation or economic integration.

"*If something happens today to this new centre of growth, to this fulcrum of emerging architectures in East Asia, the impact is going to be far-reaching, globally felt and globally negative. That is why ASEAN and India's cooperation and relationship has assumed a new level of importance and urgency.*"

Of all the regimes, of all the facilities and of all the new agreements that we have made in ASEAN, the multinational corporations are taking advantage more than the ASEAN companies and ASEAN corporations. There is nothing wrong with that because once we bring down the barrier, tariff or non-tariff, anybody can take advantage of it. The head of the Ford Company once said, "We do benefit from your FTA among yourselves. Not only we export more ready-built units or cars from one ASEAN country to another, but we trade automobile parts between and among ASEAN member states more than before." We hope that the Indian companies will take advantage of the new level-playing field that we have created and we hope that our SMEs will come to India to look into your 1.15 billion population or markets, to look into the growing middle class that you have.

One area in which ASEAN has benefited a great deal from the growth of India is tourism. Almost 3 million Indian tourists come to Southeast Asia every year. In Bangkok, in Singapore, in Kuala Lumpur, in Jakarta, in Bali, we see a lot of Indian weddings. And with Indian weddings there are about 300 people coming. With 300 people coming to one wedding, they stay about seven days – a tremendous source of our foreign exchange in Southeast Asia. But, please produce more weddings. Next year we will celebrate our twentieth anniversary and it would be a commemorative summit between ten ASEAN leaders and the Indian Prime Minister. Let us hope that at the twentieth anniversary at the summit we will be able to deliver a comprehensive FTA between us because so far it is only in goods. Services and investments we have not yet been able to conclude. Let us aim for that. And let us fulfil the hope of Prime Minister Manmohan Singh of by next year 70 billion.

When Mr. Manmohan Singh said, "Let us look East", he did not just mean it diplomatically. He meant it emotionally because his seat is from Guwahati, because his seat is from Assam and North-East India is naturally connected with ASEAN, with East Asia. We count on the support of the government, we count on the participation and contribution of the private sector, and we at ASEAN at the Secretariat are ready to help facilitate and promote any initiative that we could do together to fulfil the dream, the aspirations, the potentiality.

It is not just for 1.8 billion people that this vision, this dream shall come true. It is more important than that because this is a part of the new growth of the global community. If 1.8 billion people fail, it will have impact on that new status of East Asia, India and Southeast Asia included.

Shri S.M. Krishna

Minister for External Affairs, India

We stand at the threshold of twenty years of the launch of the formal dialogue partnership between India and ASEAN, which started in the year 1992, and we look forward to holding the commemorative summit in 2012 in India. It is a happy coincidence, or is it a coincidence that this two-decade period has been transformational for India, as also for its engagement with Southeast Asia. It has been a gratifying engagement for us, an engagement which has drawn strength from India's rapidly developing bilateral ties with individual ASEAN countries and from our millennia old bonds with countries and civilizations of the region.

> *"It has been a gratifying engagement for us, an engagement which has drawn strength from India's rapidly developing bilateral ties with individual ASEAN countries and from our millennia old bonds with countries and civilizations of the region."*

The words "Look East" encapsulate our renewed focus on these ties. Is there a phrase that can capture the age-old roots, cordiality and partnership that are at the heart of our Look East Policy? Historical ties of India with Myanmar, Thailand, the Malay Peninsula, Cambodia, Laos and with what was known as the East Indies - Sumatra, Java, Bali and Borneo - are well known. These ties are rooted in geographical contiguity and commonality of a multitude of other factors. It is both a contemporary need and a responsibility to nurture these natural relationships. We are committed to deepening our all-round engagement with ASEAN.

India's first free trade agreement was signed with ASEAN. This agreement will provide a further thrust to the almost twenty-fold increase in our trade with ASEAN which has been witnessed in nearly twenty years since 1990. India has undertaken a number of initiatives in line with its commitment to the "Initiative for ASEAN Integration," which is intended to bridge the developmental gap between the older and the newer, less developed members of ASEAN, i.e. Cambodia, Lao PDR, Myanmar and Vietnam.

The shift of power to Asia in this century is almost a cliché now. While such a shift may indeed be taking place, the processes involved are far more complex than what would appear at first glance. A number of new initiatives and institutions in Southeast Asia are coterminous with and contribute to this shift. On the strategic side, there is the ASEAN Defence Ministers' meeting Plus Eight process. India's participation in this forum is part of the wider paradigm shift that characterizes our Look East Policy.

The second big institutional change is the continued evolution of the East Asia Summit (EAS) process. Our Look East Policy has evolved with this process, which was born in 2005. This policy has, therefore, evolved to include the Far Eastern and Pacific regions and facilitated greater links with Japan, Republic of Korea, Australia and New Zealand. EAS further expanded at its fifth meeting in October last year to include the United States and Russia into its ambit. India welcomed this expansion which we believe will add to regional peace and security. We also believe that the existing mechanisms of EAS will remain intact with the expansion, and will be guided to a more fruitful benefit for the region.

With this backdrop of historical and contemporary wide-ranging association, how does India look beyond the first two decades of our engagement with ASEAN? There are a few vectors which suggest themselves for the future. Firstly, we need to focus on a mission for our region which is inclusive. As is known, we in India have sought to embed in our developmental experience the principle of inclusivity. These principles need to form part of international efforts as that in the end is the strongest factor for the maintenance of peace and security. Secondly, we feel that the principles of state sovereignty and non-interference in internal affairs of others must be the bedrock of our cooperative endeavours. Thirdly, diversity comes naturally to us in Asia. Respecting diversity and developing tolerance must, therefore, form the third prong of our approach.

Within this framework we must focus even more sharply in our efforts to construct an interconnected economic block. India and ASEAN can do so by concentrating even greater efforts on physical connectivity. This aspect fits very well with our own domestic priority of upgrading infrastructure. If the two can proceed in tandem, it is possible that in the space of next five to seven years we will see a dramatic flowering of India-ASEAN relations. Connectivity will enhance the potential of merchandise trade and investment agreement that have been already put into effect or are on the anvil.

> "*As we look to India-ASEAN engagement beyond 2012, we need to assiduously promote people-to-people relations. It is on the wings of these ties that the future of our engagement will soar.*"

Greater physical connectivity will reinforce intellectual inter-linkages that we have or will foster, such as our joint initiative for the revival of the Nalanda University. Similarly, the Mekong-Ganga Cooperation launched in the year 2000 is a sub-regional initiative comprising India and five ASEAN countries – Cambodia, Lao PDR, Myanmar, Thailand and Vietnam. Both the Ganga and Mekong are not mere rivers but they are quintessentially symbols of civilizations. This initiative is thus reflective of the cultural and commercial linkages among the member countries of the MGC through centuries. Members of the MGC are working to promote cooperation in the sectors of tourism, culture, education and transport, and communications.

Our enterprising ancestors created through the passage of time a most wonderful matrix of mutually enriching cultures and mutually reinforcing bonds. As we look to India-ASEAN engagement beyond 2012, we need to assiduously promote people-to-people relations. It is on the wings of these ties that the future of our engagement will soar.

H.E. Pehin Dato' Lim Jock Seng

Minister of Foreign Affairs and Trade II, Brunei Darussalam

Looking at history, Southeast Asia has always been influenced, over hundreds of years, by the two great civilisations of India and China. So, while the relationship between ASEAN and India may have only reached dialogue status in 1992 the people of Southeast Asia share a history with India that spans hundreds of years going back to a time where we traded with each other and through this trade, left many long-lasting influences to our languages, cultures, religions and even governance. The imprint of India's influence on Southeast Asia is still visible today, where we have temples like the Borobodur in Indonesia, and the Angkor Wat in Cambodia to Sanskrit words found in the languages of some ASEAN Member States.

Today, this relationship is more important than ever before. The ASEAN region has gone through a period of great change, strategically placed between the two of the fastest growing economies in the world. So it comes as no surprise to me that with this mutual growth, dialogue relations between ASEAN and India have also strengthened. As we move into the next 20 years, I foresee a region where trade,

> *"While the relationship between ASEAN and India may have finally reached dialogue status in 1992, the people of Southeast Asia share history with India that spans hundreds of years going back to a time when we traded with each other and through this trade left many lasting influences on our language, our culture, our religion and even governance."*

people-to-people contacts, connectivity and security between us will be dramatically enhanced, underpinned by the work that we are doing today.

With the establishment of an ASEAN-India Eminent Persons Group and the adoption of the ASEAN-India Plan of Action for 2010 to 2015 we have already embarked on our first steps to enhance our future cooperation both strategic and economically. But, how can we embark on a Renaissance of our Golden Age? A Golden Age when we were traders when there was a free flow of trade, a sharing of education and cultures, and interconnectivity through land and sea despite the odds and challenges of that period. We need to shift our 'mindset' to capture our past-history, to emphasize that once, we were traders, we were neighbours and we were friends. With this mindset, together, we can continue our journey into the future.

Trade Relations

Firstly, on trade relations, it is encouraging to see that we already have in place a Trade in Goods agreement and we are working towards concluding negotiations on services and investment. However, ASEAN and India must start exploring cooperation in other areas of mutual interest among them trade facilitation, small and medium enterprises, as well as the environment. So I urge officials to expedite the work already being done, and look forward to enhance cooperation in such areas that prove advantageous to both the people of India and ASEAN.

> *"As we move into the next twenty years, we foresee a region where trade, people-to-people contacts, connectivity and security between us will be dramatically enhanced underpinned by the work that we are doing today."*

ASEAN Connectivity

Secondly, more needs to be done to enhance the linkages between our regions. Last year, ASEAN embarked upon a long-term Master Plan to enhance connectivity not just between the ASEAN Member States but also with our closest neighbours such as India and China. I believe that, if fully realized, this initiative will dramatically benefit the lives of the peoples in both ASEAN and India by allowing not only the easier movement of people across national boundaries but also facilitate the movement of goods, services and investment. Next year, ASEAN Foreign Ministers plan to travel from Myanmar to Assam in India, to better understand the challenges of realizing such connectivity and so I hope that this trip will be just the beginning of enhanced connectivity co-operation between ASEAN and India.

People-to-People Contact: Nalanda University

Thirdly, supporting our economic relations is people-to-people contact. We need our people to understand and appreciate our history, our connections and to nurture the understanding required to ensure continued good relations. One good example of this is through working with our young to instill the appreciation of our close connections and links. It is therefore welcoming to see the Indian government's commitment to realize a twenty-first-century university over the remnants of the ancient University of Nalanda. This is an issue very close to my heart, and I look forward to working with India and other EAS countries to make this goal a reality.

Non-Traditional Issues

Lastly, we in ASEAN and India need to enhance our dialogue on issues of global concern such as food security and climate change. We are once again seeing the impact of this, where extreme weather patterns such as the recent floods in India have led to increasing food prices of basic necessities like onions in Brunei Darussalam. This is a stark reminder of the interdependence between us – how an event in one country can impact so many others, and it is for this reason, we need to find global solutions to overcome such challenges.

To conclude, one sees a bright future between ASEAN and India. However much needs to be done; and our discussions over course of the next few days will lead to not only a better understanding of the challenges but great ideas to overcome them.

H.E. Mr. Kasit Piromya

Minister of Foreign Affairs, Thailand

The concurrent hosting of the renowned Delhi Dialogue III on the subject matter entitled *Beyond First 20 Years of India-ASEAN Engagement* and the ASEAN-India Business Summit is a reflection of the very important role of the private sector in the India-ASEAN relationship. Both events demonstrate India's sense of purpose, seriousness and determination to forge further the linkages between the Indian subcontinent and a greater India.

In 2012 ASEAN and India will commemorate twenty years of our dialogue partnership. However, our relationship today has been rooted in our shared cultures, affinity and philosophies for over thousands of years. The ancient civilization of India is one of the two major Asian civilizations that have shared the way of life of the people in the present mainland and the archipelagic Southeast Asia, the region which is soon to be transformed into an ASEAN community.

> *"The concurrent hosting of the renowned Delhi Dialogue III on the subject matter entitled Beyond First 20 Years of India-ASEAN Engagement and the ASEAN-India Business Summit is a reflection of the very important role of the private sector in the India-ASEAN relationship."*

Before we discuss how we would envision the third decade of our relations, let us look back to understand where we came from and how we got here today. In the past two decades India has undergone a profound change in its socio-economic structure. From a state planning economy to a private sector led economy India has unlocked its potential in all dimensions. With its transformed economic regime, India has created one of the world's largest middle classes with immense consumer power and entrepreneurship. We now see India's GDP has gone up at the rate of nearly two digits per year. Many Indian companies are listed in the top 500 leading global companies. Many Indian entrepreneurs have not only become multibillionaires among the top richest people of the world but their visions and advices are listened to and sought after worldwide.

As the cradle of Asian civilization from time past, India has become a vibrant modern nation taking the lead in the world IT software business. India's Bangalore today has become home to world class IT companies. In another dimension, India's pharmaceutical industry has also reached out to a large number of hospitals in the world with its high quality medicines at affordable prices for all. The growth and strength of India have occurred within the context of political liberalism, openness, inclusiveness, and tolerance. What has made all of this possible?

Key factors behind modern India's success are probably not new to all of us here. However, it should be useful for emerging economies of ASEAN to learn from India and apply India's experiences to our own development models. India's success lies in its investment in people, empowering them with modern education, science and technology in particular. This smart investment has created a solid foundation for India's innovation and an outburst of creativity and new entrepreneurship with IT business as its nucleus propelling the Indian economy today.

Among others, English proficiency is another important factor that makes India the most preferred destination for outsourcing contracts of the developed nations. Its large English-speaking population has attracted outsourcing services in telecommunications, legal and other fields that earn India a lot of foreign exchange income. Also we should not forget that Indian diaspora, 20 to 25 million people of Indian origin, who live all over the world contributing doctors, engineers, diplomats, scholars, scientists, business executives, artistes, journalists, skilled labour and ordinary people, to the economies of countless nations. They have not only brought back wealth and reputation to their homeland but have also changed the way the world sees Indians and hence India.

Indian people, India's greatest resource, are at the heart of the re-emerging India today. Let me repeat once again, it has been proven to all of us that India's long march to success has always been in the framework of democracy one that is based on secular and inclusive principles.

Why has India undergone economic transformation in a very robust and exemplary democratic setting? ASEAN members of ten nations today have embraced market-based economy. Politically not all ASEAN members have become democratic states as yet. But in 2009, ASEAN together has been able to set up the ASEAN Inter-governmental Commission on Human Rights. In January 2009, ASEAN Free Trade Agreement has come into force for six original members and will be effective for all ten members by the year 2015.

> *"Over the past two decades, India's strong commitment towards integration with ASEAN and East Asia has brought India closer to our region as a key partner in the ASEAN-centred regional architecture. A reconnecting between ASEAN and India is helping to create a more open, prosperous, peaceful and stable Asia."*

From a region marked by ideological divide during the Cold War, ASEAN is now a rule-based community of ten nations united with a common purpose. With a 600 million population and a combined GDP of 1.5 trillion US dollars and now a single market, ASEAN has become the attractive region to be reckoned with. It was unfortunate that ASEAN and India's paths did not converge during the Cold War despite many centuries of close historical and cultural links. Not until India under Prime Minister Narasimha Rao embarked on its Look East policy and ASEAN at the same time embarked on its Look West policy did our paths re-converge. This meeting of minds led to ASEAN-India Dialogue Relations in 1992, the creation of BIMSTEC in 1997 and the Mekong-Ganga Cooperation in the year 2000.

Over the past two decades, India's strong commitment towards integration with ASEAN and East Asia has brought India closer to our region as a key partner in the ASEAN-centred regional architecture. A reconnecting between ASEAN and India is helping to create a more open, prosperous, peaceful and stable Asia.

The meeting today is held at an opportune time as we are about to embark upon the commemoration of the twentieth anniversary of ASEAN-India relations in 2012. It is an opportunity to explore a new direction of our strategic partnership to ensure that ASEAN-India relations will continue to be one of the cornerstones of the ASEAN-centred regional architecture.

ASEAN has now placed on top of its agenda enhanced ASEAN connectivity as it sees efficient connectivity will help accelerate the binding of an ASEAN community. It will lead to economic progress of member states and economic empowerment of communities and peoples throughout ASEAN. Sound connectivity will contribute meaningfully to the building of a more competitive and resilient economy. Yes, we have realized that enhanced connectivity cannot be achieved by ASEAN alone. ASEAN success owes its large part to our being open and outward looking. The Master Plan of ASEAN connectivity, adopted last October by ASEAN leaders, is just the first step to a broader connectivity linking ASEAN with South Asia, East Asia and beyond. The success of ASEAN connectivity will depend on creating a partnership within and outside the region. We, therefore, need the active engagement of our dialogue partners and external partners in ASEAN's strategic goal of enhancing regional connectivity.

In this regard we appreciate India, one of our major dialogue partners who shares with us both land and maritime borders, for its continuing contributions in the development of transportation networks between South Asia and ASEAN. The efforts based on India's vision to create an arc of advantage for our region through further integration of road, rail and sea links, complements well with ASEAN Master Plan on connectivity to build a seamless Asia.

India-ASEAN connectivity means a connection between our peoples of over 1.8 billion combined not only physically but intellectually and culturally.

Connectivity based on positive elements such as past historical relations, feeling of affinity, familiarity and commonalities will inevitably lead to a flow of flourishing economic activities, tourism, people's travels and contacts, academic exchanges. In this regard we welcome wholeheartedly the revival of Nalanda University, and Thailand will render its fullest cooperation.

However, to pursue our goal towards developing seamless connectivity between our two regions and peoples we need good and efficient infrastructure both in the hardware and software components. For the hardware component India and ASEAN are now accelerating the task to complete the Thai-Myanmar-India trilateral highway linking the Northeastern region of India to ASEAN via Myanmar and Thailand. Extension of this highway eastwards to Lao PDR and Cambodia is also on our agenda.

> *"It is proposed that India and ASEAN explore the possibility of kick-starting our twentieth anniversary in 2012 by making a survey trip from ASEAN via Thailand and Myanmar to Assam in the northeastern region of India. This trip, to be undertaken at the Ministerial level will symbolize our joint efforts to push forward a closer ASEAN-India connectivity and that will reinforce the new partnership between ASEAN and India."*

ASEAN is also supportive of the development of the Mekong-India Economic Corridor connecting the Mekong region to India on its eastern coast via Ho Chi Minh city, Phnom Penh, Bangkok, Dawei and Chennai. This project is being studied by ERIA with the support of India and Japan. On Thailand's part we are building roads to the Thai-Myanmar border which will eventually link up with the Dawei port, thus opening an economic corridor to the Andaman Sea which should well complement the envisaged Mekong-India Economic Corridor. With our efforts to develop these transport corridors into economic corridors, there will be much more spin off benefits to the people along the corridors in terms of economic opportunities, better access to jobs, education and health care.

In this connection, it is proposed that India and ASEAN explore the possibility of kick-starting our twentieth anniversary in 2012 by making a survey trip from ASEAN via Thailand and Myanmar to Assam in the northeastern region of India. This trip, to be undertaken at the Ministerial level will symbolize our joint efforts to push forward a closer ASEAN-India connectivity and that will reinforce the new partnership between ASEAN and India.

On the software side India could share with us its world renowned IT expertize to help improve ASEAN ICT connectivity. Such expertize will enable us to truly connect Southeast Asia and South Asia and beyond with the development of digital technology and IT software to facilitate transportation and enhance cyber linkages, thus facilitating efficient cross border management.

The entry into force of ASEAN-India Trade in Goods Agreement since January last year has created an enormous integrated ASEAN-Indian market of almost 1.8 billion people with a combined GDP of US $2.70 trillion. This partnership will enable both India and ASEAN to be less dependent on traditional markets. It now rests upon all of us to expedite the negotiation on trade in services and on investment promotion and protection.

We have also at the same time to engage our private sector the real engine of trade to capitalize on the opportunities arising from the agreement. Raising the public and private sectors' awareness is, therefore, key to implementing the FTA as well as making the fruits of economic progress accessible to our peoples.

The partnership between ASEAN and India will lend stability and dynamism to the emerging regional architecture based on existing ASEAN led arrangements. As our region is increasingly confronted with many non-traditional security challenges such as transnational crime, terrorism, natural disasters, food and energy security, we need to work very closely to address these issues and to coordinate our joint efforts at the regional and global fora such as G20, EAS and at the United Nations. We, therefore, look forward to the continued constructive role of India, and in fact the leadership of India, in the expanded EAS building on its contribution in both the ASEAN Regional Forum (ARF) and the ASEAN Defence Ministers Meeting Plus. We are also offering the Utapao Naval and Airbase as the rapid deployment centre for the disaster management.

India is re-emerging not only because of its impressive GDP growth but also its growing roles and responsibility in regional and international arenas. India's longstanding role as a leading contributor to United Nations peacekeeping is well recognized and commendable as ASEAN is also raising its profile and contribution to the UN peacekeeping efforts, the experiences of India could be shared with the ASEAN countries. Also we would like to thank the Indian Navy for rescuing some of our captured for ransom fishermen around the Somali Sea.

The peaceful rise of India will benefit the region and the world making India's partnership indispensable for ASEAN. Together, ASEAN and India can jointly shape a more balanced and dynamic regional architecture. The next steps in the growing ASEAN-India partnership as part of the evolving regional architecture will be crucial. Our meeting today marks the start of these next few steps. With support and our common efforts, if we move on all of these challenges, we will be able to move together to a very successful outcome.

H.E. Dr. Mari Elka Pangestu

Minister of Trade, Indonesia

The theme for the Indonesian Chairmanship of ASEAN this year is *The ASEAN Community in the Global Community of Nations.* The first priority is to ensure implementation and realization of the ASEAN community by 2015. This is all about implementation because we already have a blueprint. We are targeting free flow of goods, services and investment, freer flow of capital and movement of professionals within ASEAN. Obviously there is a lot of homework there but really the focus is on implementation and this includes implementation, of course, of the ASEAN-India FTA as well as ensuring that it will include services and investment. But in our recent discussions we also recognized that achieving equitable ASEAN which is actually the third pillar within the ASEAN Economic Community should receive serious attention as well as being able to deliver on some of it beginning this year.

We feel strongly about narrowing the development gaps between the lesser developed countries in ASEAN – mainly Cambodia, Myanmar, Laos, and Vietnam to some extent and the other six countries as well as within each ASEAN country. Without ensuring that the needs of narrowing the development gaps are addressed, we

> *"In terms of the regional architecture the issue has always been how to expand our ASEAN Plus Ones and our ASEAN regional architecture without losing the centrality and the relevance of ASEAN."*

cannot really progress further on the regional integration.

Connectivity and infrastructure is another important area to achieve progress and it is not just physical infrastructure, also ICT connectivity, people-to-people connectivity and institutional connectivity. In the economic sphere it means that customs, for instance, have to be harmonised to facilitate the flow of goods.

Though a lot of examples were given about land connectivity, let us not forget maritime connectivity. Otherwise we are going to leave out Indonesia and the Philippines. Whether it is building bridges that will link us to the mainland part of ASEAN and India or its maritime transportation, maritime connectivity must be improved.

> *“In terms of consolidation, the ASEAN perspective is ‘let us adopt a building block and pragmatic approach’. One can build blocks based on issues, such as consolidation based on trade in goods or consolidation based on membership.”*

The second priority of the Indonesia Year is the role of ASEAN in shaping the emerging regional architecture and the role of ASEAN in the global fora. In terms of the regional architecture the issue has always been how to expand our ASEAN Plus Ones and our ASEAN regional architecture without losing the centrality and the relevance of ASEAN. We are in a situation where everything is evolving. We have got the ASEAN Plus Ones and we have also got bilaterals between the ASEAN countries and the dialogue partners as well. So, here the challenge is to implement in a maximum way the utilization of the existing ASEAN Plus One FTAs, expanding them to a comprehensive economic partnership. That is the full marriage. FTA is just the engagement. If we want to talk about full marriage in economic integration, we have to have the comprehensive economic cooperation that includes services and investment. In addition to the equitable growth as an ASEAN goal, it should also include economic cooperation and capacity-building. This is the challenge ahead – expanding but making sure that it is balanced and inclusive, and at the same time consolidating the ASEAN Plus Ones.

And for the East Asia Summit, which will include Russia and the US for the first time in November, what is going to be on the agenda? Is it just political and security issues? What are the priority economic issues that should be on the agenda? What should be the mechanism of discussion? Should there be follow-up and how should that mechanism be? These are some of the crucial questions that are coming up. The role of India and ASEAN within that is obviously very important.

In terms of consolidation, the ASEAN perspective is 'let us adopt a building block and pragmatic approach'. One can build blocks based on issues, such as consolidation based on trade in goods or consolidation based on membership. These are some of the challenges ahead.

Finally on the global role, what should be the role of ASEAN within the global fora? ASEAN is the only regional organization that has been invited to the G20 meeting. This is a very important recognition of the role of ASEAN. The role of ASEAN within G20 is very important in outlining the position of ASEAN as well as for the trade and economic area obviously in the WTO and in the regional fora such as APEC.

There are very good initiatives within ASEAN which can contribute to some of the global issues. One example is the ASEAN+3 Chiang Mai Initiative, which is cooperation in reserves that, hopefully, will be operationalized and implemented this year. This is preventive policy as well as something one can draw on in time of financial crisis. And it can be linked to the IMF facilities which are now available in a more flexible way.

There is another idea that we have had in the food security area. There is already a plan, ASEAN Plus 3 Emergency Rice Reserves. That will be the same idea like Chiang Mai where if you have a disaster or if you have an emergency one can draw on these rice reserves when faced with disaster or emergency. This will help to tide over any food situation, which, if not handled carefully, can have a spike or fluctuation in the food prices.

The last priority is to begin a dialogue on the future of ASEAN – ASEAN beyond 2015. Given we have already the foundations laid out, what is next for

ASEAN beyond 2015? This will mean building greater connectivity, having a more equitable ASEAN and a more people-centred ASEAN.

> *We really need to design on the economic side a comprehensive economic agreement that includes liberalization, facilitation, and economic cooperation which will include capacity-building, ensuring we bring along the lesser developed countries, bring along the lesser developed regions and segments of our population so that they are benefited from the regional integration.*

We have a serious commitment for ASEAN-India engagement beyond twenty years. We really need to design on the economic side a comprehensive economic agreement that includes liberalization, facilitation and economic cooperation. This agreement should include capacity-building, ensuring we bring along the lesser developed countries, bring along the lesser developed regions and segments of our population so that they are benefited from the regional integration because, we believe, without that we are not going to have a successful regional economic integration. This will require good programming, good planning and identifying the needs that need to be addressed in a very well-designed way. Obviously it would include services, investment and other areas of cooperation to make it really a comprehensive agreement. It should include cooperation not just G-to-G but B-to-B (business-to-business). The ASEAN-India Business Council (AIBC) must play a much greater role in B-to-G as well as P-to-P (people-to-people). There comes the role of think tanks, the importance of networking between think tanks, and greater flow of tourism. The Indian External Affairs Ministry has invited thirty media people from ASEAN to join this forum. That is excellent. This is all about a greater understanding between us because at the end of the day that is really what will make us have a long-lasting commitment, long-lasting relationship. We hope that this dialogue will give us good recommendation and input so that there will be many outcomes and deliverables coming out in the next twenty years of good engagement and marriage.

LOOKING TOWARDS 2012 AND BEYOND

Amb. K. Kesavapany

Shri Anand Sharma

Dato' Dr. Mahani Zainal Abidin

Mr. Rodolfo C. Severino

Mr. Kavi Chongkittavorn

Amb. K. Kesavapany,
Director, Institute of Southeast Asian Studies, Singapore

In the years 2011-12, the world economies have recovered from the global financial crisis of 2008-9. The feared double-dip recession has not occurred largely due to many stimulus programmes put in place by various governments, notably the US and China. The EU has addressed the crisis efficaciously. Asia continues to be the world's fastest growing region led by China and India with high growth rates of 9-10 per cent. The US economy, too, is growing well at around 3 per cent.

The world's top leaders in the USA, China, EU and India look set to face challenges either via elections or through planned leadership. These changes may smooth transitions in general policies. It may continue on a steady course with emphasis on economic growth and on addressing on-going global issues of climate change, nuclear programmes, North Korea, Afghanistan, the Middle-East and other lingering issues.

> *"The development gaps within ASEAN need to be addressed urgently if the three ASEAN communities are to be realized within the timeframe set."*

ASEAN will be more conscious of the looming deadlines for the setting up of the three ASEAN communities in 2015 – in economic, security and socio-cultural sectors. The development gaps within ASEAN need to be addressed urgently if the three ASEAN communities are to be realized within the timeframe set.

Between the various accreditation powers, the widening gaps between China, Japan, and India, despite good annual growth rates of around 8 per cent, will continue. China can be expected to achieve eye-catching, spectacular feats in space science, education and economics and will remain the pace setter for Asia and the world. However, there is also an existential need for Asian countries to lift the most vulnerable parts of their populations out of poverty. What skewed income distribution can do has been dramatized in the Middle East. Unless Asian countries are eager to follow the Middle-East example, they should pay heed to the pain and anger of those at the bottom.

In terms of global institutions, it can be expected that the continuing reforms in international bodies such as the World Bank and IMF will reflect the growing clout of China, India, Brazil and others. Though Doha Round can be expected to limp along as the major economies are cautious not to jeopardize still fragile global growth, there seems to be a renewed attempt to see if the Round can be concluded this year. Major weather changes such as extreme floods and storms will convince global community that climate change is real, but progress at the Annual Conference of Parties on Climate Change will creep sluggishly due to the challenges of funding and technology transfers.

In conclusion, although much will appear to be the same over the next two years, there are actually major political and economic shifts occurring under the radar.

Shri Anand Sharma

Minister of Commerce and Industry, India

Today is the third day when we are meeting with our friends and partners from the ASEAN countries. Each in itself underscores the significance that we attach to the evolving relationship that is going to have a defining influence in the twenty-first century. It is not that India and the Southeast Asian region are getting to know each other for the first time. We have not been strangers in history. For centuries, there has been exchange of cultures, values and thoughts. Those linkages clearly convey shared heritage, shared values and shared aspirations.

Now, we are talking about retracing the old routes where our traders used to travel, the historic sea routes carrying people, and commodities. That is one part of history. But we are also trying to inform the present generations about what rich cultural exchanges had taken place in the past and how intellectually and spiritually developed our countries have been. For the initiatives in recent years, the Nalanda University initiative is a very important step which is jointly taken together. And we have the eminence of Dr. Amartya Sen as the first Vice-Chancellor. Equally important is the BIMSTEC initiative and also our common quest to ensure better connectivity and linkages between people and institutions.

The cultural footprint goes beyond the geographical boundaries of India and of other countries of the region. That is why it is a shared heritage and culture right up to Angkorwat.

We had the first meeting in Delhi of the ASEAN Economic Ministers with India, along with a business conclave and a fair. It is not merely the stalls of the industries, but our handicrafts and handlooms, showcasing the creativity of the people of the ASEAN as well as India. There is an engagement that is not only confined to formal meetings but also intellectual exchanges and vibrant cultural linkages.

When we look at the contemporary world, in the context of the changes taking place in the world, it is true that there is no decade in the last century which does not have a story of its own to tell. But, the last few decades have transformed the world in which many of us were born in. We grew up when the world was still talking about the destruction of World War II, the emergence of new countries, particularly India, which triggered a wave of liberation movements and decolonization in Asia and Africa. There were two blocs – called ideological or military blocs, the NATO and the Warsaw Pact – one led by America and other led by Russia. But, it all changed and there has so much happened in one decade: connecting the world, bringing down barriers, opening new opportunities, particularly for the generations which were born in the 1980s and the youth of today.

Whether it is symbolism of the collapse of the Berlin Wall and, thereafter, the emergence of countries of Southeast Asia, and Korea, described as economic powerhouses and the miracle economies. That decade also saw a wave of technologies – information technology, communications – shortening distances when it comes to flow of capital, flow of information. India also embarked on the path of economic liberalization and economic reforms. And we looked at the world to build strong partnerships, enduring ones for the coming decades and for the future. We have travelled a long distance as have the countries of the ASEAN region. Today, the dialogue is a continuous process which ensures that

> “*It is in the interest of the global community at a time when the world is interdependent and interconnected, when opportunities and challenges are equally shared, that the global architecture, both political and economic; reflect the contemporary realities of the world.*”

achievements will have a meaningful impact in changing the lives of people, economies and role in the changing global architecture.

Today's world as we know is different from the orders which emerged and the institutions, both the United Nations and the Bretton Woods institutions. That order is frozen in the past but the world has changed. Therefore, it is in the interest of the global community at a time when the world is interdependent and interconnected, when opportunities and challenges are equally shared, that the global architecture, both political and economic; reflect the contemporary realities of the world. India has been consistently saying this. Together we have to achieve this.

It is not for the first time in the context of our post-Independence history that India has sought to embrace its brothers and sisters in the ASEAN region. India's first Prime Minister Jawaharlal Nehru, at the time of India's Independence spoke about the Independence movements in Southeast Asia, in Asia and the struggle against colonization and oppression in Africa. First important conference convened in New Delhi was the Asia Relations Conference. Later on, he was one of the pioneers as a global statesman for convening the Bandung Conference in 1955.

It was important that the nascent independent nations had a platform and a voice of their own. Today, India and ASEAN have a relationship which has evolved into a partnership, not only economic but of strategic importance given the geographical location, the strength of the economies, the human resources. Next year, India will be hosting the ASEAN-India Summit to commemorate the tenth annual summit – the first which India will host and for which Prime Minister Dr. Manmohan Singh will invite all the respected Heads of States and Governments of ASEAN to India. We hope that summit will come out with the roadmap how to accelerate engagement to do together for the larger economic integration of Asia.

Today, Asia is demonstrating capacity and creativity of its people. More than half of the economic growth of the world comes from Asia. That resilience was acknowledged by the world during the worst economic crisis seen in last six decades. The previous ones were confined to regions, and the big developed economies including the United States of America were there to provide support, interventions, fiscal stimulus to stabilize those crises of the past, whether it happened in our region, or in Mexico or other parts of the world. This time, the crisis had come riding on top of the financial crisis. It was preceded by two major crises and challenges – the food crisis and the energy crisis. Both were back with a vengeance last year itself.

Our economies rebounded quickly. Most of us never went into a negative growth when there was a major contraction in Europe and Americas. It was serious because this time the contagion had just erupted from the heart of the capitalist world. Even today when we talk of the recovery, recovery is uneven and weak. Universality was there with the crisis and with the recovery too. But, there are many question marks particularly with what happens in some of the economies where they are confronted with the challenges of the sovereign debt. And that makes our growth story more important for the world itself.

Today, all analysts are talking about what is happening in Asia. We are home of 45 per cent of the world's population. But, the mindset has been to save and invest more. China's growth model is different from India. China is today the largest manufacturing exporter in the world having overtaken Germany. We have a model with a huge domestic market and domestic consumption. India produces, consumes and saves a lot. So, our countries have the highest saving rates in the world and that is why there are resources to invest in the economies. Fortunately, our parents never taught us to live heavily dependent on the plastic money and credit cards. And that is strength.

India has a saving rate of about 35 per cent. These are the strong fundamentals of our economy. Our national investment rate is also 34 to 35 per cent. Same is the case with other countries of the region. We look at the diversity, the richness but also the richness of the resources. We have virtually everything that needs to grow. And how we look at Asia? If we look from Middle East, from Egypt, up to Tokyo, then we have to take into consideration the presence of another very powerful country, very rich in resources – the Russian Federation. In the next couple of years, less than two years, the GDP of Asia, EU and America will be equal-sized, each contributing 25 per cent to the global GDP. And as we know, in the coming decades three of the first five economies of the world will be the Asian economies. They will be China, India and Japan. These are the strengths, and it is a partnership which will have a defining influence in this century.

India has consciously, along with its partners, tried to build strong linkages by entering into regional and bilateral economic and trade agreements. On 7 August 2009 India had signed CECA with Korea. We were questioned at that time that given the global economic situation if that was a wise thing to do. But, our Prime Minister and I have been of this consistent view that the leadership of governments is tested during a period of crisis. Historically, the tendency has been to look inwards, to go in for protectionism but the need is to dismantle the barriers, step out and engage more. That is the only way to ensure economic growth and recoveries. And within a week, we were in Bangkok for signing the India-ASEAN Free Trade Agreement. Though, we are proceeding slowly, but we definitely know that we are headed to have CECA between India and ASEAN by concluding an agreement on investment and services.

The discussions with the ASEAN Economic Ministers in Da Nang, in Hanoi, and in Delhi have been very reassuring about the commitment. We are trying to ensure that whatever remaining gaps are, we are able to close them. We did sign with Japan, on 16 February 2011 a Comprehensive Economic Partnership Agreement and within 48 hours of that we were in Kuala Lumpur to sign a highly ambitious Comprehensive Economic Cooperation Agreement with Malaysia. We are engaged now in negotiations with Indonesia and Thailand. We already have one with Singapore in place, and the second review is on.

So, this gives a very clear picture also about the sincerity of our commitment to ensure that this partnership grows from strength to strength. There has been integration of economies in the regional context elsewhere in the world – whether in Americas or in Africa, both at the pan-African level and regional level. In Asia, we are learning from ASEAN because that has been the shining example of what cooperation means. Therefore, ASEAN and the dialogue partners, ASEAN + 6, should be working together. Once we have the Comprehensive Economic Partnership Agreement with East Asia and reaching right up to the Pacific, this will be perhaps one of the most powerful economic zones in the world.

> "*The demographic dividend is going to propel our economies forward because young people have their dreams and aspirations.*"

We are at the take off point and this decade will matter a lot when it comes to growth. Our working together on new technologies will matter. We have advantages, having invested in institutions and in our people. We are home to a very large number of young people. India has 17 per cent share of the global population but 20 per cent of the world's children live in India. Two-thirds of our population are young. Same is the case with the demographic profile of the ASEAN countries. The demographic dividend is going to propel our economies forward because young people have their dreams and aspirations. Today's youth have access to better institutes of learning, and technologies. We seek to build societies in India and elsewhere which are knowledge-based and knowledge-led because there cannot be anything more empowering than knowledge and technology.

So, let us work together and fulfil the objectives that we have in mind and build a future which is secure, prosperous, and where dreams are not only dreamt but also realized.

Dato' Dr. Mahani Zainal Abidin

Chief Executive Officer, Institute of Strategic and International Studies, Kuala Lumpur

The strong relationship that ASEAN and India have forged over the years is based on the context of mutual respect and regionalism. The signing of ASEAN-India Trade in Goods Agreement in August 2009 signifies a greater venture in economic and trade relations. Despite being hit by the 2008 Great Recession, India's trade with ASEAN surged from US $39.08 billion in 2007-08 to $45.34 billion in 2008-9. As the fourth largest trading partner for India, bilateral India-ASEAN trade has the potential to reach US $70 billion in the next three years from US $50.1 billion in 2010.

> *"ASEAN and India must work together to help the world to continue to grow strongly for this year. Therefore, the first thing that we should do is to continue to deepen our trade relationship."*

The institutional cooperation between India and ASEAN encompasses various capacities in political, security, economic and social-cultural relations. India has been actively participating in a series of consultative meetings with ASEAN, including the ASEAN Regional Forum (ARF), the Post Ministerial Conferences (PMCs), ASEAN+1, East Asia Summit (EAS), Mekong-Ganga Cooperation and Bengal Initiative for Multisectoral Technical and Economic Cooperation (BIMSTEC) and Treaty of Amity and Cooperation in Southeast Asia (TAC). The strong commitment shown by the Indian

Government is evident from the appointment of H.E. Mr. Biren Nanda as its Ambassador to ASEAN in 2010.

There are no shortcuts in forging closer ties between ASEAN and India. The recent visits by leaders of both sides signify the hardwork and commitment above the members of the private sector and government officials. One can be confident of the potentials in expanding the dialogue partnership between India and ASEAN as we move towards the twentieth anniversary of ASEAN-India dialogue relations in 2012 with a Commemorative Summit in India.

Post-Economic Crisis and Forging Closer Relationship between ASEAN and India

The 2008 Great Recession has become synonymous with leaders and economists who study the magnitude of the crisis and suggest radical ways to overcome it in the future. Dialogues such as these represent a common place to reflect on the rise of China and India, as well as their potentials in being the next economic powerhouse of the century.

Coupled with India's stable democratic political system, huge middle-class population, immense military presence in South Asia, rising economic fortunes and global ambitions make it a potential power that could play a very important role in world affairs. The Indian retail market is massive as it offers direct access to disposable incomes of the much sought after Indian middle class.

In the area of human capital development, India's total population of 1.2 billion people has an immense resource of experienced, high-calibre professionals in all spheres of knowledge and technology. ASEAN must strategically place itself between India's development equation towards becoming an economic powerhouse to stay relevant and competitive.

> *“India is very well known for its vast wealth of resources in terms of educational capacity and knowledge and certainly ASEAN can benefit a lot from those exchanges.”*

The Indian economy grew at more than 9 per cent in 2004-8 before slowing down to 6.8 per cent in 2009 as ripples of the economic crisis hit domestic demand. The government's aim of becoming the world's fastest-growing economy within four years will set a benchmark for other economies, particularly ASEAN members, to cooperate and integrate our successes better for a more sustainable growth for both regions.

Given the wide range of agro-ecological setting and producers, Indian agriculture is faced with a great diversity of needs, opportunities and prospects as its future growth depends on rapid, more widely distributed and better targeted policies. ASEAN can play a role by sourcing its palm oil and rice to cater India's growing food consumption.

India is witnessing a transition from agriculture-based economy to a knowledge-based economy of Information Technology and IT-enabled services industry. Services account for 55 per cent of India's gross domestic product (GDP), while exports from the sector were valued at US $93.7 billion (Ringgit Malaysia 291 billion) in 2009. In view of this and India's competitive advantages in terms of cost and expertise, such increased access will be very beneficial. However, both sides need a more pragmatic approach in dealing with the services and investment negotiations under the ASEAN-India FTA.

Since the 1990s, ASEAN-India relations have seen a distinct rise in firm measures to integrate and cooperate in the economic as well as political spheres. As they move towards a greater context of closer partnership, India can take advantage of ASEAN's potentials as a production base (springboard) to a much larger East Asian markets, such as China and Japan. This holds ample opportunities to establish a stronger relationship with a long-term emphasis on greater cooperation and integration, alongside the robust economic, socio-cultural and strategic ties.

Challenges ahead of India-ASEAN Relationship

The 2008 Global Recession has left a significant mark in the widening global income gap between the haves and the have-nots. A new survey by the World Economic Forum says its members see widening economic disparities as one of the two main global risks over the next decade (alongside failings in global governance). Pushing exports alone would be inadequate to recover from a crisis. The balancing act of economic power between the East (China, Japan and India) and the West (US and EU) will be a critical issue as it demands a cohesive structural and corporate governance reforms.

Despite various measures by the US Federal Reserve's (aggressive actions, tax cuts and stimulus spending) and EU's (€60 billion from ECB and €250 billion from IMF in the European Financial Stability Facility) against widening trade deficits, high unemployment rate and sovereign debt defaults, recovery from the 2008 Great Recession is perceived as slow and weak. A more aggressive reforms agenda and greater political push will act as catalysts toward a sustainable economic growth.

The recent Arab world 'uprising' complicates the journey towards global economic recovery and stability. Uncertainties over the *global oil supply* have nearly doubled the price of crude oil since bottoming in late 2008. However, the significance of the event to the energy market – a major factor in the global economy – extends beyond the oil price. The post-uprising effect may result in other possible *geopolitical risks*, such as change of government policies and relationship with other world superpowers, particularly the US and EU.

The lingering after-effects of the financial crisis, climate change/natural disaster (draught, flood and earthquake) and the Arab world uprising are amongst the factors behind increasing trend of global *food prices* to dangerous levels. According to a recent report from the World Bank, its food-price index rose 15 per cent between October 2010 and January 2011 – led by wheat, sugar and edible oil – and has pushed 44 million more people into extreme poverty. Food security across the Middle East region has become more of a prominent issue of late. If current trends persist, they will likely to bring plenty of political instability in their wake.

Areas to Look Forward to 2012 and Beyond

As we move beyond greater integration process and economic cooperation, ASEAN and India must not depend only on the declining economic trends in the US and EU as a basis for growth. It is imperative to equip ourselves with possible steps for institutional reforms and mindset change in order to be competitive and relevant to the business communities. For India, ASEAN presents one avenue to diversify its relationships in the face of Beijing's growing influence in the region. However, the objective of closer ASEAN-India ties would not mean to contain Beijing's economic advancement, but to jointly manage its rising profile in the region in a peaceful, progressive and constructive way.

Under the ASEAN-India FTA, the conclusion of services and investment negotiations is long overdue as ASEAN has been demanding a single offer for all its members, whereas India insists on making a different offer for each country. As such, there is a pressing need for a greater understanding and tolerance between ASEAN and India in services and investment negotiations. Globalization is imminent, and both sides would risk being sidelined by other economic giants who foresee a strategic collaboration in the international arena.

> “*ASEAN and India can look at the issue of how to shape the agenda of the EAS and how the EAS can not only deal with economic issues but other issues of importance to the world.*”

India's continuous support for the East Asia Summit (EAS) as an open, inclusive, transparent and outward-looking forum would bring a set of common agendas for the Asia Pacific region.

Mr. Rodolfo C. Severino

Former Secretary-General, ASEAN and Head, ASEAN Studies Centre, ISEAS

There have been thousands of years of linkages between Southeast Asian countries and India. Often we have noted the alienation of India and the ASEAN countries in the early years of Independence. But in the light of the long history of linkages between Southeast Asia and India, this alienation constituted only a small aberration or a glitch in the relationship between the Southeast Asian countries and India. This alienation consisted of the political and the economic aspects.

Politically, during the Cold War there was a difference in outlook even among the neutral members of ASEAN and India. This difference in outlooks was highlighted sharply in the different approaches to for example the Vietnamese occupation, the incursion into Cambodia and its occupation of that country during the 1980s. Economically, India before the 1990s was inward looking, state-controlled and state-driven. ASEAN on the other hand by the late 1980s began shift from import substitution, state-driven economies to market-driven economies and market-oriented ones. But in the long view of history, this divergence was the blink of an eye.

> *"Almost all the FDI of India in ASEAN is made up of investments in Singapore and about half of the tourism from India to ASEAN is directed at Singapore. So, it is up to the ASEAN countries to make sure that this relationship is more evenly distributed."*

Second, the free trade arrangements that have proliferated in this region have both less and more than the written provisions suggest. They are less in the sense that it may be wrong to attribute the rapid rise of economic relations between India and Southeast Asia to the FTAs, the CECs, the CEBs and similar arrangements. The rise of trade for example is due to market forces rather than to the conclusion of these specific arrangements. But, they are also more than the provisions suggest. They are more than purely economic. They are political instruments basically and they are sending signals of a political nature, meaning signals of the good relations between, for example India and ASEAN, signals of the determination on both sides to strengthen those relations and signals also of the opportunities that can be had for profit between one country on the one side and the region on the other.

> “*Some steps should be recommended for enriching and strengthening the relations between ASEAN and India. One is to step up military and defence exchanges between the two sides. Another is a larger Indian presence in the South China Sea.*”

Third, we have talked about the rapid expansion in trade, investments and tourism between India and ASEAN. That is all true except that if you look more deeply into the data on trade, investments and tourism between India and ASEAN, you will find that almost one/third of the trade between ASEAN and India is accounted for by Singapore. Almost all the FDI of India in ASEAN is made up of investments in Singapore and about half of the tourism from India to ASEAN is directed at Singapore. So, it is up to the ASEAN countries to make sure that this relationship is more evenly distributed. And it is the responsibility not of India, or Singapore, but of the rest of ASEAN to make sure that this happens.

There are several channels which we need to exploit in strengthening our relations between ASEAN and India. The channels are indicated in the plan of action. As several speakers have noted there will be a commemorative summit in India for commemorating the anniversary of the dialogue relationship between ASEAN and India. There has already been appointed an eminent persons group for India-ASEAN relations. There is a Round Table, there is a

Delhi Dialogue, and there is India link up with the senior officials meeting on transnational crime as well as with the ASEAN senior officials on drugs. So, there are many channels which we can use for developing the mutually beneficial relations between ASEAN and India.

Finally, in addition, some steps should be recommended for enriching and strengthening the relations between ASEAN and India. One is to step up military and defence exchanges between the two sides including port calls by military vessels. Another is a larger Indian presence in the South China Sea – not in terms of siding with one claimant or another in the conflicting maritime claims or of any notions of containment or balance of power, but as a manifestation of India's abiding interest in peace and stability in its immediate neighbourhood, the freedom of navigation and overflight on which India's and other's external commerce increasingly depends, and the prevalence of the rule of international law in the pursuit of maritime claims. India, a nuclear power in all but name, can express more forthrightly its support for the Southeast Asian nuclear weapons free zone. There could be more active cultural exchanges in the light of the long history of cultural interaction between us, the Southeast Asian countries and India. Finally, the mutual updating on the respective commitments under the 2010 plan of action to carry out the partnership agreement between India and ASEAN would help to strengthen the relationship between them.

Mr. Kavi Chongkittavorn

Assistant Group Editor, Nation Media Group, Thailand

India-ASEAN relationship is like a rollercoaster. Just a couple of decades ago in 1975 and 1980, India refused to have dialogue with ASEAN because India at that time considered ASEAN as the imperial west. In 1981, when the whole world shunned the People's Republic of Kampuchea, India was one of the few countries which recognized Phnom Penh. So, it had completely frozen ASEAN relations for almost a decade. And being intuitive and pragmatic, India out of nowhere in the year 2003, acceded to Treaty of Amity of Southeast Asia Cooperation. But, India just made a twist without honking the horn and then became the inner sanctum of ASEAN by signing the Treaty of Amity. That is the best Indian diplomatic move that I have seen in the past twenty years until today.

It is yet to see what India's next major step will be in the next twenty years. The problem with India is that it does not follow suit. After 2003, China has made like 100 miles of way, but India stay put. For example, last night all the Ministers said that we have booming tourism industry, that almost between 2 and 3 million Indians are visiting ASEAN countries and only a fraction of them visit India, about less than 10 per cent, about 200,000. India has come up with a visa regulation beginning this year giving visa on arrival to the Philippines but they forgot Thailand, Singapore, Malaysia.

> *"It is the Indian exceptionalism that creates headaches in our relations."*

Being India, they give privileges to underdeveloped countries of Southeast Asia not knowing that the major crux of the group that comes to India come from Thailand, Malaysia and Singapore. So, it is the Indian exceptionalism that creates headaches in our relations.

This Indian exceptionalism has already created problems. India needs to do something about the no nuke treaty of Southeast Asia. A comparison with China tells us why India lacks imagination. For example, the plans of action between India and ASEAN and between China and ASEAN are worlds apart. China-ASEAN Plan of Action has 27 pages. India-ASEAN has only 11 pages and it reads like children's stuff. The paragraph related to Southeast Asia Nuclear Weapons Free Zone, merely states that India supports the Southeast Asia Nuclear Free Zone. But the Chinese express strong support towards realization of a Southeast Asia nuclear free zone and reaffirms its readiness to cite a protocol to the ASEAN no nuke treaties, together with ASEAN nuclear weapons as soon as possible. India merely maintained its support for the implementation of this nuclear free zone as an effective instrument towards the promotion of international peace and security. China was the first to inform ASEAN that it was ready to accede to the SEANWFZ treaty. It was ASEAN who is trying to slow down China. India has signed the Treaty of Amity and Cooperation in 2003 but has not yet started on the SEANWFZ. On the other hand, America signed the Treaty of Amity last year and within one year, it has emerged as one speaking on behalf of ASEAN, on almost anything, on freedom of navigation, freedom of internet. India as the world's largest democracy is still keeping quiet, waiting for its opportunity. It is going to wait for another twenty years.

Even though India has the level-playing field, it does not use it. India can make a jumpstart by saying that it is ready to accede to treaty of no nuke Southeast Asia, because Southeast Asia is going to discuss this in East Asia Summit. In East Asia Summit, we will talk about

"*India can make a jumpstart by saying that it is ready to accede to treaty of no nuke Southeast Asia, because Southeast Asia is going to discuss this in East Asia Summit.*"

nuclear non-proliferation treaty. Of course, India is not part of it. You can still talk about the civilian nuclear pact, the so-called CTBT. And this is a very good chance for India to make a jumpstart to show to ASEAN that India really is on the same page with ASEAN, to show that we are real partners.

“*Bollywood is yet to produce a* 3 Idiots *Part II, with a Thai idiot or a Malaysian actress. This is very important because it is through this kind of soft culture one can learn to appreciate India once again.*”

There exists similar level of ambiguity over the issue of supporting human rights protection mechanisms within ASEAN. The Foreign Minister Kasit Piromya referred to this mechanism and mentioned that India has never pledged any support by giving any funds. At the moment, all the human rights related activities of ASEAN come from Sweden, Switzerland, the Netherlands. Why cannot India contribute? India should be able to do something to promote democracy within ASEAN framework. And it is not a taboo subject. In the China-ASEAN Plan of Action 1.6, China has offered to cooperate, to promote human rights in ASEAN. We are waiting for India to offer assistance to ASEAN. So, this is another area in which India needs to take an initiative. ASEAN already has a human rights body which India can help. India has the moral authority as a democratic nation and human rights to help us.

Third, and this is one of the most serious things, is about the soft culture of India. There is a little India in every Southeast Asian country. We were raised with Indian movies. Now, the whole Thailand has been overwhelmed by the so-called Korean wave. The problem is India has no imagination of using the Southeast Asian actors and actresses. The movies in South Korea are using Southeast Asian actors and actresses. Bollywood is yet to produce a *3 Idiots* Part II, with a Thai idiot or a Malaysian actress. This is very important because it is through this kind of soft culture one can learn to appreciate India once again. Otherwise people just overlook India.

Finally, the Indian media seldom reports about Southeast Asia. It is done only when we are in deep trouble especially Thailand made good news with all the 100 TV channels here. There should be increased exchanges of media between ASEAN and India. One keeps wondering why there are more ASEAN journalists trained in Germany than in India? One fails to know why Germany can be so concerned with media development in ASEAN and not India. There are so many scholarships from Germany for Southeast Asians but there are none from India. In these areas there should be exchange, strengthening co-operation of news networks and also explore ways to TV co-productions. Recently China has obtained rights of sitcom and translated it into Chinese. The Chinese think that for them to co-exist with their southerners, they better understand Thailand's sitcoms and not a new novel from Mexico or somewhere else. So, it is about time that this kind of cooperation permeated into Indian theme Southeast Asian sitcom. It is in this kind of non-sensitive spheres that we can learn and appreciate each other.

INDIA-ASEAN CONNECTIVITY

Amb. Ong Keng Yong

Shri C.P. Joshi

H.E. Mr. Kasit Piromya

Datuk Seri S. Samy Vellu

Mr. R. Ravindran

Mr. Hidetoshi Nishimura

H.E. Mr. U Nyunt Maung Shein

Amb. Ong Keng Yong

Former Secretary-General, ASEAN and Director, Institute of Policy Studies, Singapore

---

Let us begin by making three important points about ASEAN. First, ASEAN has completed the three "Cs" and has moved into the fourth "C". ASEAN is building the envisioned Community based on the three pillars of political/security cooperation, economic integration and socio-cultural cooperation. ASEAN has brought the ASEAN Charter into force and this has strengthened accountability and the rule of law necessary for the realization of the ASEAN Community. ASEAN has adopted the Master Plan on Connectivity to link up the different parts of ASEAN and to bring the peoples of ASEAN closer to one another.

After "Community", "Charter" and "Connectivity", ASEAN is now focussed on "Corridors". These are the economic development initiatives to open up designated areas for business, industrial and social advancement through infrastructural upgrading, regulatory reform and expanded networking with other similar locations. Several economic corridors have been planned or implemented in ASEAN and the surrounding countries such as in India. The challenge today is to make them more inter-connected and efficient in moving the respective economic agendas forward.

> "*It is only by connecting with the people around us and with the big powers which are interested in our region that we will become much more prominent and significant in the global terms.*"

The second point about ASEAN is its collective approach and cohesiveness in managing common challenges. Member-states of ASEAN may be arguing with one another or are having bilateral disputes with each other but they would coalesce as a group to achieve common strategic goals. When they do so, they would be in a hurry to achieve the desired results and this could come across as ASEAN being "impatient". For example, ASEAN wishes to conclude the chapters on trade in services and investment of the ASEAN-India FTA as quickly as possible. The global and regional conditions are favourable to a comprehensive free trade accord between ASEAN and India with substantial mutual benefits to be gained.

Thirdly, ASEAN Member States are aware that Southeast Asia may be bypassed if the region is not economically competitive and not well connected to the other important economic nodes around the world. In the early 2000s, FDI flows into ASEAN were declining as investors flocked to the other emerging economies elsewhere. Therefore, ASEAN strives to be open, outward looking and connected with other countries and regions. ASEAN is committed to adding value to its relationship with its Dialogue Partners and those having an interest in the region. ASEAN has developed several mechanisms for economic, political and strategic cooperation to preserve regional peace and security.

Let me say a bit more about the ASEAN Connectivity initiative. The Master Plan on ASEAN Connectivity was adopted by the ASEAN Leaders at the 17th ASEAN Summit in October 2010. The Master Plan highlights the key strategies and actions (with stipulated timelines) within the three pillars of physical, institutional and people-to-people connectivity. The adoption of the Master Plan demonstrated ASEAN's continued commitment to its 2015 economic integration and community-building goals. ASEAN's next challenge is to muster the political will and financial support necessary to implement the Master Plan. It was envisaged that ASEAN would seek the support of all its Dialogue Partners and other international agencies and development partners to realize the vision of ASEAN Connectivity.

To facilitate the implementation of the Master Plan, an ASEAN Connectivity

Coordinating Committee (ACCC) would be established. The Terms of Reference (ToR) for the ACCC was finalized in Ho Chi Minh City in December 2010 and endorsed by the ASEAN Foreign Ministers in Lombok in January 2011. In addition to the ACCC representative, each ASEAN country is expected to nominate a national coordinator to oversee the implementation of specific plans and projects in the respective ASEAN countries. The ASEAN Secretariat would also establish an ASEAN Connectivity Unit to monitor the implementation of the Master Plan.

In line with the implementation of the Master Plan, an ASEAN Foreign Ministers' Connectivity Roadtrip took place from 23 to 25 January 2011, where the foreign ministers travelled along Route 3A of the North-South Economic Corridor from Chiang Rai, Thailand, to Kunming, China through Laos. This was followed by the ASEAN-China Foreign Ministers' Meeting which discussed future cooperation in enhancing ASEAN-China connectivity.

Going forward, the ASEAN Leaders have committed their governments to work with ASEAN's Dialogue Partners to effectively implement the Master Plan. ASEAN and India can work together through ASEAN-centric mechanisms such as the East Asia Summit (EAS) to improve connectivity. Other than China, India is the only EAS Dialogue Partner which shares physical land borders with ASEAN. ASEAN would like to encourage India to be actively and substantially involved in ASEAN Connectivity. A fully integrated ASEAN would benefit the EAS. It would fully realize the potential of ASEAN's network of FTAs with ASEAN's Dialogue Partners, including the ASEAN-India FTA. The implementation of the Master Plan will be a complex undertaking and ASEAN looks forward to the continued support and commitment of its EAS partners for the connectivity projects.

ASEAN could look at ways to dovetail the India-Myanmar-Thailand-Laos-Cambodia Highway with the ASEAN Connectivity initiative. For example, India may also wish to consider linking up with the ASEAN Highway Network or the Mekong-India Economic Corridor.

To help familiarize themselves with the state of land connections in the region, the ASEAN Foreign Ministers are looking at undertaking a road trip from Myanmar to Assam, India, in 2012. The road trip will also be an opportunity to celebrate 20 years of dialogue partnership between ASEAN and India. ASEAN seeks India's support for this project, which will be the third road trip after similar undertakings in 2010 (from Thailand to Vietnam via Laos) and 2011 (from Thailand to China via Laos).

Shri C.P. Joshi

Minister of Road Transport and Highways, India

India and ASEAN are not just maritime neighbours but we also share a land boundary of 1,600 kilometres with a member state of ASEAN that is Myanmar. In the two decades since the establishment of Indian Dialogue Partnership with ASEAN, we have progressively expanded our functional exchanges to cover a wide range of areas including human resource development, space sciences, science and technology, health, transport and infrastructure, small and medium enterprises, tourism, information and communication technology, agriculture, energy, support for initiative for ASEAN integration and people-to-people contacts.

Recently, we have taken a number of initiatives which will further strengthen our dialogue partnership and functional exchanges in the years to come. We have drawn out a plan of action for the India-ASEAN partnership for the period 2010-15 that lays down the roadmap for cooperation over the next five years. We have agreed to establish an Eminent Persons' Group (EPG), which will develop a vision for our partnership over the next decade. The progress in our dialogue partnership and functional cooperation is contingent on our continued ability to strengthen

> *"The progress in our dialogue partnership and functional cooperation is contingent on our continued ability to strengthen physical, institutional and people-to-people connectivity between India and ASEAN."*

physical, institutional and people-to-people connectivity between India and ASEAN.

For physical connectivity, there are several challenges to be addressed to improve the poor quality of roads and incomplete road networks, missing rail links, inadequate maritime and port infrastructure including dry ports, inland waterways and aviation facilities and the growing demand for power. This calls for the upgrading of existing and construction of new infrastructure and logistic facilities, the harmonization of regulatory framework and innovative techniques.

India shares a land boundary of 1,600 kilometres between Myanmar and the north-eastern states of India. Myanmar plays the role of a land bridge between India and ASEAN. It is for this reason, India has been working with Myanmar and Thailand to strengthen road and rail connectivity between India and ASEAN. Among several road projects undertaken by India, the most significant one is the 160 kilometres India-Myanmar Friendship Road in 2001 on the Myanmarese territory from Tamu to Kalewa.

> *These projects are an important element of India's endeavour to build physical connectivity to ASEAN and to reach out to Southeast Asia.*

Other projects in the pipeline include the construction/upgradation of Rhi-Tiddim and Rhi-Falam road section in Myanmar. Similarly, Yangon-Mandalay trunk line will also be upgraded with the Indian assistance. The Kaladan multimodal transport project is another proposal for connectivity which is being undertaken by India in Myanmar. The project involves a major upgradation of the infrastructure at Sittwe port located about 250 kilometres from the Indian border on the coast of Myanmar where Kaladan River joins the Bay of Bengal. The objective of this project is to achieve physical connectivity between Kalewa in Myanmar and National Highway 54 in Mizoram. The trilateral highway projects between India, Myanmar and Thailand under the Mekong-Ganga Cooperation Initiative begun in 2005 is an attempt to promote road connectivity between the three countries, which expands trade, tourism and people-to-people contacts.

The trilateral highway of 1,360 kilometres to be built at the cost of US $700 million will connect More in India with Mae Sot in Thailand through Bagan in Myanmar. The Friendship Road and the Trilateral Highway will become vital sections of the designated Asian Highway running from Singapore to Istanbul and passing through Myanmar and India. These projects are an important element of India's endeavour to build physical connectivity to ASEAN and to reach out to Southeast Asia. We are also currently considering developing a new India-Myanmar-Laos-Vietnam-Cambodia highway.

Railways are an extremely cost effective and convenient mode for the transfer of goods and people. India is currently working on railway projects like Jiribam-Imphal-More line in the northeast Indian State of Manipur and the Tamu-Kalay-Segyi line in Myanmar as well as the rehabilitation of Myanmar's existing Segyi-Chaungu-Myohaung line. These projects are estimated at the cost of US $649 million, US $296 million and US $62.5 million respectively. These rail linkages will ultimately dovetail into the Delhi-Hanoi rail link proposed at the MGS Ministerial meeting in Phnom Penh in June 2003. However, much work needs to be done to bring this link into reality and need to be laid out for completion and operationalization.

Air connectivity is a vital aspect of physical connectivity between India and ASEAN. At the second India-ASEAN summit, the then Prime Minister of India, Mr. A.B. Vajpayee offered a partial open sky policy outside bilateral aviation pacts for Southeast Asian airlines under which they would be free to operate daily flights from ASEAN capitals to Indian metropolitan cities. This unilateral move taken by India was a result of a realization for better connectivity between India and the ASEAN.

India and ASEAN are now engaged in discussion on a full open sky policy. A Joint Working Group has been established to work out details of an India-ASEAN air transport agreement. The policy when implemented will introduce a paradigm change in the air connectivity between India and ASEAN. The Economic Research Institute of ASEAN and East Asia has been working on a comprehensive Asian development plan which envisages three infrastructure-cum-industrial corridors. One of these corridors is Mekong-India corridor which will link Cambodia, Lao, Vietnam and Myanmar to the eastern coast of India. We strongly endorse and support the efforts of ERIA to plan and bring the infrastructure to reality. The Mekong India Corridor when realized will lead to a surge in the creation of multi-country infrastructure, freight corridor and a centre of industrial activity. This will in turn empower and enable intra-regional production chains giving a boost to regional economic integration and economic activity.

"The Mekong India Corridor when realized will lead to a surge in the creation of multi-country infrastructure, freight corridor and a centre of industrial activity. This will in turn empower and enable intra-regional production chains giving a boost to regional economic integration and economic activity."

To achieve institutional connectivity and enhance movement of goods between India and the ASEAN, we have implemented an India-ASEAN Trade in Goods Agreement and are currently negotiating a Trade in Service and Investment Agreement to complete the India-ASEAN FTA. ASEAN is a major trading partner for India and accounted for over 9 per cent of India's global trade in 2009-10. India's trade with ASEAN amounted to US $47 billion during 2009-10 registering a sevenfold increase in the bilateral trade volume of US $6.6 billion during 2001.

We hope to achieve a trade volume of US $70 billion with the ASEAN countries by 2012. With the India-ASEAN FTA in place, growth in trade in the future should be even higher than wheat we have achieved in the recent past. The India-ASEAN FTA is to be supplemented with bilateral FTAs with individual ASEAN countries. India signed a Comprehensive Economic Cooperation Agreement with Singapore in 2005. We have completed negotiations on bilateral FTA with Malaysia last year. This year we hope to conclude an FTA with Thailand and a Comprehensive Economic Cooperation Agreement with Indonesia.

For two thousand years, India and Southeast Asia have been linked by close cultural and commercial ties. India has taken several initiatives to reinforce our historical people-to-people connectivity. Recently we have extended visa on arrival scheme for the nationals of Cambodia, Vietnam, Philippines, Lao PDR, Myanmar and Indonesia to facilitate easier movement of nationals of these ASEAN member states to India. We are negotiating an India-ASEAN Tourism Cooperation Agreement which will pave the way for enhanced tourism between India and ASEAN. The India-ASEAN Joint Working Group on tourism has identified several cooperation activities including visits by Buddhist pilgrims to India and preservation of World Heritage Sites in some ASEAN countries. India has also been providing scholarships for ASEAN students to pursue their higher studies in the Indian educational institutions.

At the last India-ASEAN Summit, Prime Minister offered IT scholarships and expanded youth exchange programmes between India and ASEAN. We have active cultural exchanges with ASEAN countries. Our age-old historical ties and cultural links are reflected in common elements in our language, religion, social customs and rituals, literature, performing arts and the visual arts. We need to reinvigorate these links and remind our youth of our common heritage of culture and shared values. Enhancing connectivity will be the key to realizing the long-term goals and aspirations of India's dialogue partnership with ASEAN.

H.E. Mr. Kasit Piromya

Minister of Foreign Affairs, Thailand

We believe that we could really make the realization of the connectivity for the whole of Southeast Asia both on land, sea and by air and from Southeast Asia as a connecting point to the West, namely to the Indian subcontinent and also across the Bay of Bengal and up the Northeast into China, Mongolia, far-eastern Russia and to the two Koreas and to Japan as well as to Taiwan. Such a firm belief of the possibility of world connectivity requires explanation.

Almost fifty years ago we children were taken by our school to see the Thailand-US Friendship Highway in the northeastern part of Thailand. It was in the 1950. It was such an excitement for the first time for any child from the developing world or from Thailand to be able to witness a sort of a four-lane super highway by America in Thailand fifty years ago.

After that, that particular island for the first time opened up the whole hinterland of Thailand namely Northeastern Thailand. With that we were able to grow rice especially at the tide for export. Tapioca was being sent in the form of pellets to the Netherlands at 8 million tonnes a year for thirty years. Then we became also one of the

> *"India trying to make 20 kilometres a day, 7,000 kilometres in a few years' time to connect the whole of the Indian subcontinent, and it makes the Asian highway of forty-fifty years ago a dream becoming reality."*

major producer and exporters of cane, sugar, other fuel crops, fruits, vegetables and so on and were able to go to the globalized market because of that one particular friendship highway between Thailand and the United States. That opening up of the hinterland did lead a lot to the socio-economic development of the whole country. That has always been at the back of the mind when we talk about road connectivity, that friendship highway.

Russia, Central Asian countries, China and so on are going to make three or four superhighways across Central Asia to reconnect once again the roads. After that, we also have lingering suspended concept about the Asian Highway from Lebanon to the western Pacific shores. That is still in the making at the UN ESCAP headquarters in Bangkok. At the same time, the Asian Development Bank has been trying to alert everyone. Subsequently, we set up a high-level working group for a master plan on connectivity which was adopted by the ASEAN leaders last year.

We have talked to every dialogue partner of ASEAN. The Indian government picked it up; the Chinese picked it up and so on. Subsequently, the dream became a reality, and last year the ASEAN countries set up the ASEAN Infrastructure Fund. We are financing it ourselves. The Asian Development Bank, the World Bank and major financial institutions from Japan, the Chinese EXIM Bank and so on, are ready to provide concessionary loans financing for the less developed ASEAN members. Things are becoming more and more of a reality. Last year, ASEAN and the world heard about India trying to make 20 kilometres a day, 7,000 kilometres in a few years' time to connect the whole of the Indian subcontinent, and it makes the Asian highway of forty-fifty years ago a dream becoming reality.

A few weeks ago, there was the meeting of the Economic Cooperation Organization (ECO), an organization of Central Asia with Iran, Pakistan, and Turkey. They also have agreed on a couple of highways that would connect the western part of Asia, Central Asia to the eastern part of Asia into China, into India and into Southeast Asia. Not only the road transportation but the pipelines also would go east-west and also from Central Asia down to Afghanistan into Iran and into Pakistan and so on. In the past twelve months, there has been so much of activity all over Asia and now connectivity is not a dream but becoming a reality more and more everyday.

On top of that, each of the countries in ASEAN, in the Indian subcontinent, in China and so on has come up with its own individual internal budget to upgrade and improve on the infrastructure. The individual undertaking, sub-regional and regional undertaking, wider regional undertaking and the intra-regional undertakings are ongoing at the moment. We can look with a sense of optimism that within ten years it would be fun to be able to drive from Singapore and face a choice if we want to turn left or turn right or go up north into Mongolia. It is no longer a dream but very much a reality. In this sense, we are ready to play a part.

Two years ago, Princess Sirindhorn headed a Thai delegation and we took a train ride across the Mekong River into Laos. It was for the first time ever that Laotian people would now be able to be connected to the South China Sea to Thailand by land because Laos is a landlocked country. We wish the Laotian people to be able to travel across the Mekong River either by car or by rail to the warm sea in Southeast Asia. Now, Japan is also trying to make a super railway networking North-South right down to Singapore. We hope that we could have also the East-West connecting from Vietnam into Laos, Myanmar, Thailand, Bangladesh and into India, and take the railroad.

Datuk Seri S. Samy Vellu

Malaysia's Special Envoy to India and South Asia on Infrastructure

With a combined population of 1.8 billion and GDP of US $2.75 trillion, India-ASEAN business relationship is one of the largest free trade areas in the world. It offers a huge prospect for both ASEAN and India to reshape the global economy collectively. Over the last decade, we have seen Asia emerging as a new engine for growth of the global economy. ASEAN has become an essential player with a market size of over 600 million people, and an accumulated GDP of US $1.5 trillion. The time is now ripe for India and ASEAN to capitalize on the partnership through an enhanced connectivity in order to reap the benefit which would in turn provide a win-win scenario for both India and ASEAN.

The India and ASEAN community are connected through people-to-people connectivity, trade connectivity and infrastructure connectivity. There are no less than 7 million Indians who reside in the ASEAN region and their roots can be traced back to India. This is the foremost relationship that warrants bilateral engagement between India and ASEAN. At the same time, it can be said that 600 million people of ASEAN will start to view and perceive India

> *"The time is now ripe for India and ASEAN to capitalize on the partnership through an enhanced connectivity in order to reap the benefit which would in turn provide a win-win scenario for both India and ASEAN."*

as a next destination for import and export of goods and services.

On the question of trade connectivity, the bilateral trade between India and ASEAN has reached an astonishing volume of US $50 billion. This alone has created an adequate opportunity for extraordinary trade, investment and connectivity for both economic mega houses. On the question of infrastructure connectivity, the presence of bilateral cooperations in the area of land, air and sea connectivity is a clear indication of a mutually beneficial collaboration between India and the ASEAN region.

There are also five areas of common interest that both India and ASEAN could interestingly strategize and deploy to gain from the unprecedented business potential that the region offers through connectivity strategies. One is the trade connectivity. With the signing of the trade in goods agreement of ASEAN-India Free Trade Agreement (FTA), which came into effect on the 1 January 2010, the trade potential of this unified economic region will create a collective trade and business opportunity amounting to a combined GDP of over US $2.8 trillion. The demand for efficient transportation and reduction in trade time, will be of prime importance for FTA which is the largest in the world. With such a potential, it is rather an important mechanism that would in turn provide the economic push to the ASEAN, and it must be agreed that a prosperous ASEAN is equally vital for India.

The open sky policy between India and ASEAN region must look beyond facilitating the movement of people between those two regions. We must now tap into the potential of global tourism market which has its landmark towards Asia and Asia Pacific. With a positive growth between 1 to 3 per cent in the global tourists' arrival to the Asia-Pacific, India and ASEAN must start developing creative travel packages that would not only enhance but would open up the tourist potential in both regions.

> “*With a positive growth between 1-3 per cent in the global tourists' arrival to the Asia-Pacific, India and ASEAN must start developing creative travel packages that would not only enhance but on that would open up the tourist potential in both regions.*”

The spiral effect towards the tourism related to upstream activities will then further spur economic engagements.

Similar potential exists in the sector of seamless telecommunication connectivity and convergence for travellers. With more than 20 active telecommunication companies in the ASEAN region and not less than five major players in the Indian telecom business, it is extremely pertinent that we jointly develop seamless voice, data and multimedia connectivity. We should provide a unified rate coupled with seamless connectivity especially for wireless broadband services. India alone has no less than 526 million mobile subscribers and with ASEAN telecom penetration rate exceeding more than 90 per cent, the potential is gigantic.

One can only envisage the business and the social interaction that would further encourage the business connectivity between both the regions. The unified Small and Medium Enterprise (SME) network and connectivity, in the ASEAN region is accounted for more than 96 per cent of all the enterprises and 50-85 per cent of the domestic employment. A similar pattern also exists in India. There is a necessity to connect this SME effectively. In order to accomplish this, both ASEAN and India ought to develop a joint vendor programme in order to promote this SME network into an inclusive economic model that would allow SMEs to collaborate and tap each others' potentials and strengths. Vertical sectors such as automobile and manufacturing would also be among the prime areas for concentration between two economic regions.

On space technology and connectivity for disaster management, India's supremacy in space technology and satellite data management is imperative for ASEAN countries which are occasionally exposed to natural disasters and which would have direct impact on the economic and the well-being of ASEAN. As close partners, both India and ASEAN could establish a space technology aided disaster management centre which would work towards providing timely connectivity and information. Such a solution can also be marketed to other parts of the world as part of India-ASEAN technology showcase.

In conclusion, in addition to the tangible economic benefits of India-ASEAN connectivity, these linkages created would intensify and strengthen India-ASEAN business, and social relationship especially through the people-to-people contacts and, move to position ASEAN and India as a key driver for the economies of Asia and to stimulate unprecedented growth rate.

Mr. R. Ravindran

Chairman,
SAEA Group Research Pte. Ltd., Singapore

Everyone should take the time to read the ASEAN Master Plan on Connectivity. It is not only an excellent piece of work, but more importantly, there is an excellent mechanism that is stated there regarding regional connectivity and methods of implementation. They not only put up a master plan but to ensure that implementation is done they put in a coordination committee. More importantly, they rank who does well and who does not do well, by putting a score card system. That is very good model that needs to be implemented not only within ASEAN but also perhaps with the dialogue partners. Sometimes some of the countries which have borders or projects involve dialogue partners. There could be a push that could be inserted whereby countries are forced to relook not only intra-ASEAN projects but also at projects involving dialogue partners and ASEAN members.

It is important that we create a mechanism whereby there is regular check and progress, and if necessary a scorecard system implemented so that there is pressure and need for countries to comply with this mechanism to ensure that these projects are completed on time. It is a welcoming suggestion for the ASEAN Foreign Ministers to take a route through Myanmar to

> "*India should move towards an open skies agreement with Southeast Asia as soon as possible so that this engagement between people can also take a faster pace in the area of aviation.*"

India or through Laos-Myanmar-India. They can see for themselves what the impediments are when they make decisions and decide to institute mechanisms.

Two aspects of institutional connectivity need to be highlighted. There is a decision by ASEAN to go for an ASEAN single aviation market by 2015. Unfortunately, many of the ASEAN countries do not have direct flights to India. We should have flights not only from capital cities but also regional cities. There is tremendous movement of people from India to Southeast Asia. But, it is equally important that we increase the number of visitors who are coming to India. India should move towards an open skies agreement with Southeast Asia as soon as possible so that this engagement between people can also take a faster pace in the area of aviation.

> *"India and ASEAN can also foster movement of people via tourism through the sea. Singapore, Malaysia, and Thailand are cruise centres. This cruise industry can develop into something big whereby in future we can have cruise centres in Kolkata, in Chennai, in Goa, in Mumbai and many other places in India."*

Another aspect of the connectivity report is the idea of single maritime market in ASEAN. India could do much more besides connecting ports which are in the neighbouring countries of ASEAN. India can be far more active by setting up ports in ASEAN countries. Many bigger countries in the region are coming forward to set up infrastructure projects in ASEAN. They are setting up ports, airports, and various other infrastructure projects. Some are under Official Development Assistance (ODA) but some are set up by the private sector. There has so far been hesitancy on the part of India and particularly the private sector to go into many of these infrastructure projects. There are many countries in ASEAN whether it is Philippines, Vietnam, Indonesia, which are very eager to develop infrastructure projects to ensure that they are able to not only connect within the country but connect with the region. This is an area where India can contribute and play a much bigger role.

India and ASEAN can also foster movement of people via tourism through the sea. Singapore, Malaysia, and Thailand are cruise centres. This cruise industry can develop into something big whereby in future we can have cruise centres in Kolkata, in Chennai, in Goa, in Mumbai and many other places in India. These will ensure that a greater movement of people is seen between ASEAN and India.

In the area of people-to-people connectivity, India and ASEAN have greater engagement between educational institutions and students of educational institutions. There is a sizeable number of Indian schools in Singapore, in Malaysia but in other ASEAN countries their presence is small. But, the number of ASEAN students coming to India to study is very small. Education is an area where India can contribute. In the 1970s, one of the landmark institutions in Singapore was the Tata Singapore Training Centre where they provided skills training for Singapore workers so that they could go onto do skilled jobs. In many ASEAN countries, there is a requirement for such skilled labour not only in the capital cities but also in the regional cities and outside the city areas where the people who need these skills will benefit.

In the area of educational institutions, India can also certainly send more of the higher educational institutions to set up in ASEAN countries, particularly IITs, IIMs and also medical educational institutions which are considered world class. India should take more students from ASEAN countries, train them and send them back because they are the future ambassadors for India in the ASEAN countries.

Japan in the late 1970s started a programme called 'Ship for Southeast Asian Youth' whereby they gathered youth leaders, put them together for one month on a ship, share ideas, get to know each other, and more importantly bring them back to Japan and spend about one week to ten days to get to know that country. This was an attempt to target future leaders. Similarly, if India can come out with a concept like this whereby it gets young leaders from ASEAN visiting India. When they go back, they will end up being future leaders of ASEAN and also ambassadors for you. They also bring back a rich understanding of the country and that is vital for greater understanding between the new generation and the future generation of people in India.

There is a scope for greater understanding in India about ASEAN. There is a requirement for developing greater understanding especially among think tanks and universities about Southeast Asia. It is time that more resources are put into develop scholars and researchers who understand Southeast Asia and who can go about subsequently becoming leaders, policy makers and even ministers. One of the set backs faced in Delhi is the availability of very few specialists in India who specialize on Southeast Asia and who have a good understanding. More resources need to be put in by the government. Perhaps, the private sector can come about to endow more funds to think tanks, create a bigger group of scholars who understand Southeast Asia, who even speak the language and who are able to contribute greatly to future policy making in India.

> "*India should take more students from ASEAN countries, train them and send them back because they are the future ambassadors for India in the ASEAN countries.*"

On last note, connectivity will take a bigger pace or faster pace in future and ASEAN will definitely see ASEAN community in 2015. Together with the contribution of dialogue partners like India, we sure can see a great and bright Asian century.

Mr. Hidetoshi Nishimura

Executive Director, ERIA

The most important point is the economic impact of connectivity and the best example is the Chinese miracle. China became a member of WTO in 2001. WTO offers five years to perform obligations. Between 2001 and 2006, Chinese miracle appears. That means, the Chinese domestic connectivity was completed before that. Each Province in China is independent, different, disconnected. The Chinese GDP doubled during the five years and the Chinese GDP is now the same as that of Japan.

Similarly, the ASEAN Economic Community (AEC) is a 2 trillion dollar economy in 2009, the double of Chinese starting point. ASEAN is going to complete the connectivity by 2015. That means, in ten years ASEAN's GDP will be surely double, nearly same as Japan in ten years. What is the impact of that growth? ASEAN, if it completes the AEC programme, will create 10 trillion demands. This is not just a discussion but real benefit. If China can do it, why not ASEAN?

The Indian Prime Minister, Dr. Manmohan Singh, gave a very important message in the last East Asia Summit. He said, "I would like to complement the Economic Research Institute of ASEAN and East Asia for their work in promoting regional integration by providing useful research and practical policy

> *"The new proposal is to develop the Mekong-India Corridor from Ho Chi Minh, Phnom Penh, Bangkok, Dawei in Myanmar to Chennai and more."*

recommendations on regional connectivity, trade, investment and environment. The ERIA has identified the three corridors for building the infrastructure connectivity and the industrial activity that will support the realization of a community in the region. One of these is Mekong-India Economic Corridor."

These remarks of Prime Minister Singh incarnated statement of East Asia Summit that reads, "we sixteen leaders appreciated the completion of the Comprehensive Asia Development Plan by ERIA in cooperation with the ADB and ASEAN Secretariat." So, this is officially endorsed project ratings.

One can propose a new programme of the CADP Phase II because this Delhi Dialogue is the most important forum. The new proposal is to develop the Mekong-India Corridor from Ho Chi Minh, Phnom Penh, Bangkok, Dawei in Myanmar to Chennai and more.

The objective of our new study is to investigate the progress, challenges and expected impacts of ongoing projects to enhance ASEAN-India connectivity focusing on the Mekong-India Economic Corridor and the trilateral highway between India, Myanmar and Thailand along Asian Highway No. 1.

H.E. Mr. U Nyunt Maung Shein

Myanmar's Permanent Representative (retd) to the United Nations, Geneva

Myanmar is the only ASEAN member country that shares a common land boundary with India. It also has a maritime boundary with India. Against this backdrop, Myanmar finds itself in a strategic position in the overall ASEAN-India relations. Myanmar bridges the northeastern states of India with the rest of ASEAN. It is also a conduit for the physical connectivity between ASEAN and India. It plays a significant role in the development of the hinterlands of Mizoram, Manipur, and Assam, transforming this region into a major commercial hub linking not only India and ASEAN but also India and China. While the physical connectivity through Myanmar offers vast opportunities for economic development, trade, and people-to-people contacts between India and ASEAN, it also poses major challenges and issues which need to be resolved.

First, for any land connection with India and ASEAN, well-defined and clearly demarcated international boundaries are required. The international boundary between Myanmar and India is almost demarcated except for a sector around 120 kilometres while the boundary between Myanmar and Thailand remains largely to be demarcated. The section of the

"While the physical connectivity through Myanmar offers vast opportunities for economic development, trade, and people-to-people contacts between India and ASEAN, it also poses major challenges and issues which need to be resolved."

Myanmar-India boundary which has been pending since the 1970s is important in the fact that it is located at a place where the highway from Myanmar to India passes through.

Second, concomitant with the well-defined boundaries is the prevalence of security, stability and peace in the border areas. Such condition is conducive to smooth and efficient road and rail connections. Myanmar-India border areas, the upper northwestern part of Myanmar have Naga separatists on the Indian side of the border. But, the concerned authorities on both sides are cooperating on this issue and progress has been made.

Third aspect is ASEAN-India connectivity by road through the development of the ASEAN Highway Network (AHN). A large portion of the AHN lies in Myanmar and, at present, the condition of quality of roads and highways in the country is generally poor and not up to the required ASEAN standards. Upgrading the existing highways requires capital investment which we cannot yet meet. The trilateral project among India, Myanmar and Thailand, which has been initiated under the Ganga-Mekong Initiative, is also facing some problems in terms of required financial resources. The planned trip next year for the ASEAN Foreign Ministers to travel through Myanmar to the border with India will no doubt be beneficial as the participants will be able to observe first-hand the challenges on the ground.

Fourth is the rail connection. Railways in mainland ASEAN countries use the metre-gauge. This corresponds to that of railways in northeast India. This is advantageous to both partners as the need for changing the rolling stock at the borders is eliminated. Now our Myanmar Railways Network extends from northwest of the country from Kalay to the southeast to Thambuzayat. There is some missing link between India and Myanmar and Myanmar and Thailand. Here also we are facing financial difficulties and if these are resolved we can connect these two missing links.

“*Because of the sanctions imposed by the West on Myanmar, we are unable to secure loans from international financial institutions and as a consequence we have some financial difficulties.*”

Fifth, India is now assisting Myanmar in helping develop a multi-nodal transport system which will connect Mizoram through our country to Kolkata Port. A deep sea port is being built in Sittwe in western Myanmar. Then, we have the East-West Corridor which was mentioned earlier by Mr. Nishimura, passing through Vietnam, Cambodia, Thailand and Myanmar, connecting seaport of Da Nang in Vietnam to that of Dawei in Myanmar. This will bring benefits not only to ASEAN and India but also to the rest of the world. Unfortunately, because of the sanctions imposed by the West on Myanmar we are unable to secure loans from international financial institutions and as a consequence we have some financial difficulties.

However, recently an agreement has been concluded between private sector in Thailand and Myanmar government to develop the seaport in Dawei and an industrial zone together with related infrastructure including road and rail links with Thailand. The private sector involvement is very important and private sector from both Thailand and Myanmar and maybe even beyond will be heavily involved in this multi-billion dollar project.

Lastly, the sixth point is the seamless flow of goods and people through international borders. This is necessary for timely transportation of goods and cost-effectiveness. At present, there are some impediments such as restrictions on entry of motor vehicles from territory of one ASEAN country to another, different safety standards of vehicles and driver qualifications. And also there is a lack of uniform and consistent procedures regarding customs and immigration formalities, and also visa restrictions exist. If we could overcome these formalities there will be a seamless flow of goods and people.

In conclusion, ASEAN and India through synergized cooperation must try to overcome these difficulties. One of the major points is the participation of the private sector. For instance, to construct roads or railways in our country now we are using, but this is only for the local private sector, the BOT basis. And in future we can consider participation of private sector from ASEAN and India in such ventures on the projects to develop road and railway infrastructure.

NALANDA AS A SYMBOL OF ASIAN RENAISSANCE

Dr. Gopa Sabharwal
H.E. Mr. Kasit Piromya
Prof. Tan Tai Yong

Dr. Gopa Sabharwal

Vice-Chancellor (Designate),
Nalanda International University

As we embark on the long journey to rebuild Nalanda, it must be stressed that it is through collaborative effort that the shape, form and structure of this great institution is going to be given substance and reality.

The recreation of the university with the historical legacy of Nalanda requires first of all a full awareness of the incredible legacy of the original Nalanda and the factors that made it what it was. It is a remarkable fact that the original Nalanda University lasted for almost 800 years and ended at a time when the much acclaimed universities of Oxford and Paris had just been founded and Cambridge was yet to come into being. Bologna came into being when Nalanda was 600 years old, and Al Azhar in Cairo when Nalanda was 500 years old. Nalanda is thus by far the oldest institution of learning in the world that we know of.

The legend of Nalanda, however, is not due to its age alone. It is due to the fact that it imparted organized learning for an unbroken period of nearly 800 years. Moreover, it was truly international in that it drew students from all over the region. We know from records that Nalanda had students from places like China, Tibet, Mongolia, Korea, Sri Lanka, Turkey among others. It also existed alongside a wider tradition

> "*Nalanda's greatest gift was to liberate knowledge from the narrow confines of geography or religion and seek to share it with the world at large.*"

of organized higher learning as exemplified by the existence of Odantapuri and Vikramsila in the vicinity.

Nalanda was clearly the first choice institution of its time attracting students and scholars from far and wide. Records also show us that Nalanda was not just a centre of teaching and learning, it sent out scholars and experts to various places on request to administer over debates, to set up centres, and to spread learning and enlightenment to a larger corpus of people. The most distinctive aspect of Nalanda learning and one that we cannot afford to lose sight of was that it was all about giving, dispersing and sharing knowledge. Nalanda's greatest gift was to liberate knowledge from the narrow confines of geography or religion and seek to share it with the world at large.

In the 800 years between the destruction of the old Nalanda and the current project to establish a new university with the same name, much has changed. The decline of Nalanda coincided with the shift in the notion of what constituted knowledge. And in the intervening 800 years, the nature and form of the university as an institution came to be established after some remarkable changes. The expansion in knowledge led to yet another change namely the emergence of new branches of science and scholarship, a process that only increased as time passed.

In fact, such was the situation by the twentieth century that it became difficult for any single university to include within its ambit, within the ambit of its disciplines, all the new branches of learning and at the same time retain the hallmark of the university which was a community of scholars and scientists with specialized skills. In consequence, the progress in the branching of new specialisms and the increase in disciplines has led to the development of new kind of universities, one of which is the emergence of the specialized university concentrating on law or agriculture or education, etc., a far cry from the original idea of a university being a coherent unit covering a full range of academic engagement from philosophy to medicine.

India itself did not see the emergence of another university after Nalanda until 1857 when the three Presidency universities were established by the British. The encounter with the modern university in India albeit through a new language was also marked by the encounter with Western thoughts and ideas and an exposure to new subjects and approaches. It also had other consequences in terms of social significance. The university in India has done more for the emancipation of women that any other institution. They not only prepared women for entry into the work spheres equals with men, but also allowed more than any other institution men and women unrelated by kinship to interact freely. The university also allowed similar interaction between people of different castes and communities.

This juxtaposition of history and current reality is the ground situation that we face as we work to lay the foundations of a new university. Nalanda has the opportunity to break the mould and chart a unique course. We must not forget that Nalanda is a work in progress and will only get better with time and experience as ideas strengthen and Nalanda grows.

> *"The new Nalanda is envisaged as an open, secular, inclusive institution. It will stand for developing an orientation to modern knowledge with a tradition of the original in mind. There will be an academic focus not only on Asia and the interconnections between Asian regions but also between Asia and the world."*

The Nalanda University was established by a special Act of Parliament in August 2010 and has formally come into being as a legal entity on 25 November 2010. Nalanda is a stand-alone autonomous international university. In February, the University has been handed control of 446 acres of land in Rajgir at an approximate distance of 10 kilometres from the site of the original Nalanda. There are many aspects to building a university and logistics are of course going to be just as important in this project as the more fundamental questions about the kind of university we should have at Nalanda.

The new Nalanda is envisaged as an open, secular, and inclusive institution. It will stand for developing an orientation to modern knowledge with a tradition of the original in mind. This is why along with the original concerns of history, philosophy, comparative religion and literatures, the new Nalanda also has modern intellectual concerns like ecology and environment, peace studies, information sciences and technology, and development studies.

Nalanda is starting small with seven schools at the postgraduate level. These schools have not been chosen at random. Thought has gone into both the contemporary and the conventional and the nature of their interconnection. Our current challenge is to carve out a unique academic character for ourselves, one that will allow students, faculty, and researchers to pursue knowledge and learning in an inter-disciplinary setting. The international character of the university will be our first challenge.

Lord Meghnad Desai, Member of the Governing Board, has said in the vision statement adopted by the university, "Both students and faculty must be chosen for their desire for and capacity to absorb knowledge in diverse fields. It must have, as it did before, the best scholars and researchers. It must afford them a vibrant living environment, which will also nurture the next generation, the children of those creating knowledge." The focus on academic excellence is central to the project and is something that cannot be diluted. Nalanda will harness the best talents not only for the creation but also dissemination of new knowledge as well as for the recovery and restoration of valuable old insights. In doing so, there will be an academic focus not only on Asia and the interconnections between Asian regions but also between Asia and the world.

Turning once again to the Vision Statement of the university, it says, "A university of the third millennium has to be universalist in its outlook, open to currents of thought in practice from around the globe and it has to respond to the needs of a world which has miles to travel before it can ensure peace and prosperity with equity and hope for all the people of the world." Our current mission is to find ways to convert this mission into reality. The vision of Nalanda is that it will be a place that should become a champion of international harmony, peace, toleration and cooperation. It should reflect, strengthen and forge inter-Asian and other interactions and promote mutual understandings between Asian peoples. It is fortuitous that as Nalanda becomes a concrete reality, we are currently witnessing in Asia a replay in modern times of something that has been on since ancient times. In that era we know that Nalanda was a central part of this great interconnection which in those times too spanned intellectual, religious, cultural and material spheres.

This great connection between India and its neighbours on all sides got eclipsed by history for a while but is being revived now. Nalanda University wants to regain its central position in this network for we must not forget that in the past if there was an idea that united the geographical area we call Asia, Nalanda was central to it.

Along with other linkages that bound India with other regions, the educational link of Nalanda built bridges and created understandings with regions with whom we are once again forging meaningful partnerships. In the global world that we inhabit now, the interdependence of Asian countries visible through the flow of labour, capital and knowledge, is vital for the success of all concerned. There is a need for this interdependence to be recognized at all levels including intellectual. And Nalanda University will be in the forefront of this endeavour since this re-emergent Asia needs new ways of thinking about regional connections.

It is our endeavour to, once again, make Nalanda the natural first choice destination for all those in search of knowledge and learning. It is also the hope of everyone involved in the project that as Nalanda grows and develops, it will share its gifts with the surrounding region, hence, promoting a seamless relationship between knowledge and the place where it is embedded, in the process, enriching the institution, the people, and the very land itself.

H.E. Mr. Kasit Piromya

Minister of Foreign Affairs, Thailand

Nalanda University is not only about the philosophy or about the teachings of Lord Buddha on how to get over the sufferings and so on but it would also be scientific in its orientation. It should be based on the principle, the teachings and the insights, into the universe and into the mankind, of Lord Buddha. If that is to be understood, it could be the pure philosophical religious side, back to the very teachings and the discourses of Lord Buddha. In that sense, the project would get very big support not only from the governments in the Asia-Pacific region but also from the ordinary people.

The support to the whole project must come from two sources – one from the government budget from the taxes of the people and second is a pure contribution of the individuals who are interested. This is how we are going to promote the revival of the Nalanda University.

There is a bit of confusion whether the Nalanda University is going to be the Buddhist studies-based and the Buddhist scientific look alone or it is going to have both the Buddhist studies as well as modern subjects of computer, science, medicine and so on. This needs to be cleared by the Indian Foreign Ministry and also by the existing Board at the moment. This is very important for securing support

> *"Though the Nalanda University should be centred in India, there should be networks and its branches outside India as well."*

of the Buddhist communities around the world. If it were to be a general university covering so many faculties and so on, the enthusiasm would somehow subside. Second, though the Nalanda University should be centred in India, there should be networks and its branches outside India as well. The physical centres of Nalanda in various cities and towns and capitals would be one, networking of the scholars would be another.

We have been hearing all along that now the Asia-Pacific would control 40-60 per cent of the world GDP and be the driving force of the global growth. We are even now venturing into changing the rules of the IMF and World Bank and the Basil 3 because all of these institutions were being very much dominated by the Western world and Western thinking. Since now we are going to be in the driver's seat, we should also change the rules to make it more conducive and more universal in appeal. In that sense and in the sense of economic and basic well-being, it would be most welcome if Nalanda University were also to be a vehicle of the philosophical changes in the world.

"*It is about time now that the Indian subcontinent or we in Asia should be leading the world not only on the financial rules, banking rules, but on the moral behaviour of mankind.*"

At the World Economic Forum, held in Davos, Switzerland in January-February 2011, the subject matters, for the first time, were not concentrated on trade, finance and banking. There were two sessions on the social values and social contract. Similarly, themes of the next Summer World Economic Forum, to be held in June 2012 in Bangkok, Thailand, would be more on the moral values of how to do the economic activities since money alone without the moral precept has got us into financial and banking crises. Through Nalanda University and through the great Indian civilization, we can also make the world moralistic and it is about time now that the Indian subcontinent or we in Asia should be leading the world not only on the financial rules, banking rules, but on the moral behaviour of mankind. The new Nalanda University should not concentrate too much on the question of the stomachs but on the beauty of the hearts and the mind.

Prof. Tan Tai Yong

Director, Institute of South Asian Studies, Singapore

By now, we all know why the Nalanda University is such an important and significant project. First, we are not talking about the building of a new university. We are talking about the creation of the modern avatar of an ancient university. This university has a glorious past. What is being built now will hark back to the glorious past. As the High Commissioner reminded us, this is not about living on past glories but on the ability to derive the symbolisms of that rich history and the place of Asia in the world of learning and how Asia had such rich antecedents that has been forgotten sometimes. Now there is a possibility to reclaim that position.

Second, Nalanda's history reminds us of the deep connectivity and regional interactions that took place in Asia, something which, all of us have been wanting to resuscitate. These antecedents have been there and the connectedness was what Nalanda symbolized at its prime. Although it had a faculty and students and scholars who were mainly Indian, it was able to attract scholars from all over the world, from China, Persia, Turkey, and Japan, to study within its vicinity. This was truly a global university and had global reach. Many famous Buddhist scholars have talked about their learning experiences in Nalanda.

> "*It is time, and, perhaps, Nalanda University will be a university well positioned to do that, to reclaim that intellectual knowledge that must be distinctively Asian.*"

Even before the word globalization or global became topical, we already saw a global university. It is a global university with an Asian core, and that is important to bear in mind. There are many modern universities in Asia now, which have adopted that symbolism of wanting to be a global university – because a university cannot survive unless it has global relevance – but at the same time to give character to the specificity of the university being located in Asia. Many modern universities are now trying to claim the Asian core. Nalanda has the Asian core already built for itself. What it now needs is to revive the past when it was really global, and to bring that form of globalization or globalism to the modern context, maintaining at the same time, its Asian core.

Third, this project to revive the pan-Asian spirit and connectedness will not only symbolize the Asian renaissance – this term has been used – but will also boost Asia's confidence in its own intellectual and academic capacities. It is time, and, perhaps, Nalanda University will be well positioned to do that, to reclaim that intellectual knowledge that must be distinctively Asian. The Asian renaissance should reflect three core values that have sprung from this region – a certain degree of openness or a willingness to learn across boundaries; the inclusiveness that should incorporate different brands and different types of knowledge; and third, perhaps a secular approach to knowledge, to life and to outlook. These are perhaps the three core values that the Asian renaissance must capture and perhaps Nalanda would give these values the right prominence.

As befitting a university that has an international core to its character, this enterprise has seen the involvement and support from many partners. This is quite heartening that it is a project that has now caught traction and there are people who are prepared to support this. Singapore's Foreign Minister, George Yeo is a very enthusiastic supporter of this project. The ISEAS and its director, K. Kesavapany have also been a very keen advocate and supporter and created the Nalanda-Sriwijaya Centre that studies interactions. It is a very important project because it will provide the historical context under which Nalanda thrived and which will remind us of how connectivity can again be achieved in Asia.

We must not underestimate the challenges that we face because we are in the enterprise of building a university and the challenges of doing such a task are formidable ones. First, there have to be resources. There is a need for governments and the people to support this enterprise because one can not build a good university without sufficient money. A huge endowment will be needed. Second, infrastructure will have to be built because scholars and students will need the wherewithal to learn to function. This infrastructure should not just be within the university campus but there must be an environment, an enabling environment beyond the campus that will support the enterprise. Third, the curriculum – we have spoken about it – must be distinctive, must be a niche. At the same time, there must be sufficient connections so that the university will not be isolated and will be able to attract the best international scholars and international students to its corridors.

ENHANCING INDIA-ASEAN COOPERATION IN CRITICAL AREAS OF NON-TRADITIONAL SECURITY ISSUES/GLOBAL COMMONS NALANDA AS A SYMBOL OF ASIAN RENAISSANCE

Maj. Gen. (Retd.) Dipankar Banerjee

Amb. Mushahid Ali

Dr. Maria Ligia Noronha

Prof. Aileen San Pablo-Baviera

Shri Amar Nath Ram

H.E. Mr. U Aye Lwin

Maj. Gen. (Retd.) Dipankar Banerjee

Mentor, Institute of Peace and Conflict Studies

There are no hard security issues between India and ASEAN, notwithstanding just a couple of points raised regarding the nuclear weapons free zone or the South China Sea. These are not issues between India and ASEAN. With India and ASEAN for two millennia and more, there never has been any aspect of hostility or conflict. We need to keep this in mind as we go along with the discussions and frame our cooperative possibilities in maintaining and ensuring non-traditional security concerns and security of the global commons.

Though we have been aware of the non-traditional security challenges, the 9/11 turned the focus away from non-traditional security towards traditional security and global terrorism and all the challenges that it connoted. Today we see the revived attention and seriousness towards the non-traditional security issues, which include a whole range of activities.

The other issue that is coming into the fore is the concept of security of the global commons. In our part of the world there is a clear understanding that a village property never belonged to individual villagers. Actually in many of the tribal areas of northeastern part of India, the entire village land did not belong to individuals but was a shared property of the whole

> *"The concept of Global Commons that there were areas which were not the property either of individuals or of nation states but that, given the rapidly globalizing world of today, requires to be equally protected and secured."*

village, and divided only for a period of time for the use by individuals and then they would revert back to the village. The concept of Global Commons is that there were areas which were not the property either of individuals or of nation states, but that, given the rapidly globalizing world of today, requires to be equally protected and secured. This idea of the global commons includes high seas, the resources under the ocean and, of course, being expanded to include issues like software. Are these properties of an individual or a nation or are they a global property, global commons?

The real challenge in South and Southeast Asia is how to address these questions, how to develop these ideas in their positive connotations and build these as bases of meaningful interaction between States and citizens.

Amb. Mushahid Ali

Senior Fellow, S. Rajaratnam School of International Studies, Singapore

The Asia-Pacific region, of which ASEAN is a central part, is in the most peaceful era in its history. It has experienced thirty years without inter-state conflict. Extraordinary economic growth has lifted hundreds of millions out of poverty. Notwithstanding this striking record, a host of long-running low-level internal conflicts continue in Southeast Asia. The same could also be said of India and other parts of South Asia.

The Asia-Pacific's growing economic dominance is reflected in the rise of China and India. By 2025 China and India will have overtaken the GDP of all states except the United States, according to a study by the Center for International Cooperation, New York University. The global financial crisis has helped boost China's and India's rise. In fact, China has overtaken Japan to become the second largest economy globally. The emergence of China and India is also recasting Southeast Asia's geopolitical landscape as both compete for energy, markets, diplomatic influence and naval access.

> *"The emergence of China and India is also recasting Southeast Asia's geopolitical landscape as both compete for energy, markets, diplomatic influence and naval access."*

Southeast Asia faces a host of pressing transnational challenges, including food, water and energy scarcity, climate change, terrorism, transnational crime, and pandemics. A number of these challenges are interconnected and can exacerbate each other, e.g. the food crisis of 2008 hit Southeast Asia hard with protests over soybean scarcity in Indonesia and government crackdowns on those hoarding rice in the Philippines. Potable water availability and trans-boundary water management are growing problems throughout the region. Along the Mekong River basin, for instance, Thailand, Laos, Cambodia, Vietnam and Myanmar are downstream of the Chinese dam projects which will control the river's flow and have a potentially dramatic effect on those countries' fresh water and food supplies.

Southeast Asia (and South Pacific) will be among the regions most affected by climate change and the attendant increase in the number and strength of natural disasters. The Asia-Pacific broadly defined, is the most natural disaster-prone region. In the last 10 years, the region has experienced more than half of the world's disasters. Urbanization and high-density living in Southeast Asia make its population highly vulnerable to such events. Flooding is expected to increase in coastal areas, particularly affecting the low-lying deltaic regions in Southeast Asia and coastal Pacific island villages. Rising temperatures and rising sea levels will increase the risk of illnesses such as malaria, and likely force mass people movement throughout the region. Some of Indonesia's smaller islands and whole Pacific island states will probably be subsumed. Climate change is therefore regarded in the South Pacific as an existential threat, as it is in the Indian ocean. The effects of climate change are already being felt by the archipelagic states of Southeast Asia and the low-lying atolls of South Pacific. Storms are intensifying in the South China Sea – double the usual number of cyclones batter the Philippines and Vietnam every year.

Food, water and energy scarcity are all linked challenges and climate change will serve as a major "threat multiplier". Climate change is already exacerbating existing water problems such as the salination of the Mekong Delta. Salt water is contaminating acquifers across the region, compromising drinking water. Experts predict that climate change will also cause food shortages in the region due to lower crop-yields and declining fish populations. Climate change is expected to have major geostrategic implications such as the destabilization of state governments, the fuelling of terrorism and the mass movement of refugees and internally displaced persons.

The defence ministries of regional countries as well as major outside powers such as the United States, have to factor in climate change into their national security strategy. For instance, the naval and air capabilities are required for relief operations after cataclysmic events like cyclones, tsunamis and earthquakes. India and ASEAN countries experienced the ravages caused by the Indian Ocean tsunami of 26 December 2004. India was able to deploy 32 ships and over 20,000 naval personnel to evacuate casualties as well as provide emergency sources of power and water to the peoples of Sri Lanka, the Maldives, Indonesia, Thailand and Malaysia. The navies of those countries and India have since been taking part in joint exercises which will enhance their cooperation in meeting future challenges in these NTS areas.

> *"These transnational challenges such as piracy, resource scarcity and climate change are also opening up new opportunities for functional co-operation between both Asia Pacific and outside actors."*

Transnational threats are also likely to be among the drivers of future instability and possibly internal conflict. A major shock to a fragile state's system, e.g. from a severe pandemic or water shortage could significantly weaken governments and their institutions and overwhelm the fragile state's already reduced capacity to function. The growing food, water and energy scarcity could likewise cause an international crisis if sub-state groups come into competition over access. Threats such as water and energy scarcity have the potential to inflame inter-state tensions. The continuing drive for energy security, for instance, could cause conflict between states contesting energy-rich territory such as the South China Sea. But these transnational challenges, such as piracy, resource scarcity and climate change, are also opening up new opportunities for functional cooperation between both Asia-Pacific and outside actors. The protection of international shipping lanes from attacks by non-state actors, such as Somali-based pirates in the western Indian Ocean, has seen multinational cooperation by the navies of India, ASEAN and East Asia in combating this menace.

Terrorism Threat

Southeast Asia also faces an ongoing threat from Islamic terrorist groups with links to Al Qaeda. The threat from Jemaah Islamiyah has diminished, due in large measure, to regional law enforcement cooperation and Indonesia's policing and deradicalization efforts. However it retains some capability. The discovery of an Aceh-based terrorist training camp, and bombings in Jakarta in the past two years indicated the durability of the terrorist threat. The militant group Abu Sayyaf remains active in the southern Philippines and the Philippines armed forces continue to launch further operations against it.

Transnational crimes, including drug production and trafficking, human trafficking, money-laundering, identity fraud, is also a serious problem in the region, particularly emanating from states with weak security infrastructure and control over their territory. Laos, for example, has porous borders with its five neighbours and over recent years there has been a significant increase in opium cultivation and opium production and trafficking. Cambodia is susceptible to money-laundering as well as drug trafficking. Large-scale quantities of heroin and metamphetamines are produced in territory controlled by the *Wa* ethnic group within Myanmar and then trafficked throughout the region and beyond.

Piracy has long plagued the Straits of Malacca. The number of attacks, however, has decreased markedly over the last few years as a result of a concerted regional effort, such as the coordinated naval patrols by Indonesia, Malaysia and Singapore and supporting action by Thailand and India in the Bay of Bengal. As SARS and Avian flu showed, Asia is a likely source of future pandemics which have the potential to overwhelm the health systems of fragile states. Here too, regional cooperation such as through monitoring incoming passengers at airports has helped keep the threat in check.

Regional Cooperation

While there are mechanisms in Southeast Asia for regional cooperation in tackling transnational challenges and threats in non-traditional security areas these can be enhanced by Indian-ASEAN collaboration. The fourteenth ASEAN

Summit held in Thailand on 1 March 2009, approved the ASEAN Political Security Community blueprint. Embedded within it is the call for the intensification of counter-terrorism efforts by the early ratification and full implementation of the ASEAN Convention on Counter-terrorism which was signed in January 2007 in Cebu, Philippines. The main objective of this convention is to provide for the framework for regional cooperation to counter, prevent and suppress terrorism in all its forms and manifestations and to deepen cooperation among the law-enforcement agencies and relevant authorities of the Parties in countering terrorism. However, some argue that due to the nature and root causes of terrorism in Southeast Asia and ASEAN's principle of non-interference, the regional organization can at best only manage the threat of terrorism but not effectively resolve the problem.

Aside from intra-regional measures, ASEAN has also undertaken several external cooperation arrangements with countries such as United States, China, Japan, South Korea and Australia in 2003. ASEAN and EU also issued a joint declaration on cooperation to combat terrorism in Brussels. Both ASEAN and EU stressed the desire for a regional approach and agreed to focus their cooperative efforts on areas such as technical assistance and capacity building in regional counter-terrorism operations, border security and immigration control. In this regard India and ASEAN could enter into similar arrangements to enhance cooperation in addressing transnational crimes, such as through information exchange.

Energy Vulnerabilities

Cooperation to mitigate energy vulnerabilities is particularly important for the emerging economies of East Asia, including India and ASEAN. They are largely dependent on a limited range of external energy sources, which expose them to vulnerabilities which could affect their level of socio-economic development. Various avenues for cooperation to ameliorate such vulnerabilities could be pursued while taking into account weaknesses of existing initiatives. The existing supply of global and regional energy sources is vulnerable to two primary threats. Firstly there is the threat to adequate and secure supplies of energy at affordable prices. The increasing volatility of energy supplies has caused dramatic price changes, with serious implications for the availability and affordability of energy. This situation is essentially due to the lack of alternative supply sources. The second threat is environmental damage as a result of excessive energy consumption. East Asian countries would witness the most significant growth in energy demand, while increase in demand in the developed world would be marginal. As a result of the surge in energy consumption, carbon dioxide emissions would also go up rapidly, with China, India and ASEAN region projected to be the source of much more of these emissions than other countries and regions. The increasing dependence of Asian countries on fossil fuel imports as their economies rise is, in addition to being harmful to the environment, detrimental to their economic growth.

Effective regional cooperation would be in part dependent on the degree to which states themselves are committed to adopting energy solutions, such as introducing energy efficiency measures and investing in renewable energy sources. There is room for improved regional cooperation in tapping the opportunities available in the current evolving global circumstances, e.g. the availability of oil from the Russian Far East.

Social Impact of Changing Climate

ASEAN and India can cooperate in mitigating social impacts of climate change, such as growing migration and *modus operandi* of military organizations. They need to create policies that are informed by the push and pull factors leading to migration. They should prepare for migration as the best climatic adaptation strategy available for vulnerable populations. They should use foresight to prepare for this shift in ways that will reduce social challenges for both migrant and receiving communities.

Militaries should recognize climatic assessments emerging from the natural and social science communities and plan accordingly. Otherwise they risk being caught unprepared for the challenges that will likely accompany climate change. Military planners should pinpoint areas in which social grievances and group-identity fractures might be exacerbated by climate change and prepare to move quickly to ensure that instability and violence are effectively curtailed.

Accordingly military roles and capacities should be extended to respond to environmental threats, particularly quickly occurring phenomena such as storms and flooding, and promote lift capabilities, quick-response capabilities and disciplined organizational structures, well-placed to respond to disaster trends that are likely to become more acute with climate change.

As noted by the NTS Asia Centre in Singapore the challenges of climate change will affect societies around the world in different ways and effective policies must always be formed with the particular vulnerabilities and needs of constituent populations in mind.

(Acknowledgments to Elsina Wainwright: Conflict Prevention in Southeast Asia and the South Pacific; Center for International Cooperation, New York University, April 2010; Tuty Raihana Mostarom: ASEAN and the threat of terrorism in Southeast Asia; ICPVTR, RSIS/NTU 2010; Policy Brief on Overcoming Energy Vulnerabilities in East Asia: Ways Forward by Sofiah Jamil, Jochen Prantl and Mely Caballero-Anthony, Centre for Non-Traditional Security Studies, RSIS, February 2011; and Policy Brief on Climate Change and Security by J. Jackson Ewing, CNTSS, RSIS, February 2011.)

Dr. Maria Ligia Noronha

Director, Resources and Global Security Division, The Energy Research Institute, Delhi

The regions of ASEAN and India are exposed to a number of the non-traditional security threats and we have already enumerated some of them. It is true that we are exposed to these risks but just because we are exposed to the risk do not necessarily make us vulnerable to those risks. There are ways in which one can reduce or mitigate the vulnerability and that is what we need to work together as regions to reduce vulnerability through adaptation of which cooperation is a central plank. It is in this context that we need to look at cooperation conceptualized around non-traditional security issues as development challenges to ensure positive sum thinking and right priorities. Our responses need to be cross-border, consultative, transnational and pluralist in order to be able to think differently from the way we have been thinking of traditional security issues.

Second, global commons tend to be thought of as just the connecting media. Most of the security literature tends to talk of global commons as connecting media but they also store huge resources and that is what led to the exclusive economic zones and the whole laws of the sea debate. It is the riches that is connoted in the global commons that is now creating

> *“India and ASEAN have something that has not been highlighted in international debates, and that is institutional and social innovation capacities to deal with a number of non-traditional threats that we have.”*

pressure for regime changes. It is important that we engage with the new entrants and new players in this area to be able to understand what are their aspirations and the needs in the context of the global commons.

It is in this connection, therefore, that India and ASEAN countries need to articulate these issues – not so much as security issues but as foreign and domestic policy problems centred around vulnerability, equity and access. Cooperative action, therefore, needs to involve both behind the border co-operation but also beyond the border cooperation. Both of these have to be both inclusive and representative of emerging needs and interests. India and ASEAN already have the institutional infrastructure, institutional diversity required to address cooperation. It is just that we need to do more towards actually coming up with some outcomes.

India and ASEAN have something that has not been highlighted in international debates, and that is institutional and social innovation capacities to deal with a number of non-traditional threats that we have. These are evident in the way we have managed some of the pandemics; this is evident in the way we are looking at decentralized energy solutions; the ways that we have handled the tsunami disaster. Many of these have very interesting institutional implications that need to be highlighted in a more multilevel institutional infrastructure for sustainable development. ASEAN and India already have this institutional diversity in place to address both the non-traditional security threats and the global commons issues. What we need is to creatively link all these institutions in order to produce the desired outcomes that we need.

There are five areas of cooperation that we could focus on in order to address this. One is to invest in regional and trans-regional public goods, e.g., disaster early warning systems and management systems, disease surveillance and monitoring systems, trans-boundary water management initiatives, regional power pools, R&D in cyber security and transnational gas pipelines for the region.

Second, we need to foster partnerships between Indian organizations and the Asian Centre for Energy to create markets for renewable energy and adoption of models of sustainable habitats. We should undertake joint R&D

projects on clean coal technologies and commission policy projects on the benefits to global energy security, of energy trade between ASEAN and India.

Third, we should establish joint knowledge centres or support regional knowledge networks to work on non-traditional security issues, emerging health, both the communicable disease variety as well as the non-communicable disease variety, and governance around global commons and resources. Fourth, we can undertake research on IPRs and possible carbon barriers to trade issues to enable a better representation in Durban because Cancun really did not address this issue.

Finally, there is a need to create linkages between India and ASEAN Research Grant Councils to take up joint research between institutes and universities on a number of shared concerns and interests and emerge from Track 1, 1.5 and 2 dialogues.

Prof. Aileen San Pablo-Baviera

Asian Centre, University of the Philippines

India and ASEAN cooperation is extremely important in helping to ensure economic growth and prosperity, peace and security, sustainable development and social justice for the people of Asia. Both sides realize that economic growth is fundamentally important but does not really suffice to ensure security and stability both for the region and for the individual countries. On the one hand, to enjoy security and stability, there is a need to build mutual trust, equality, and mutual respect among nations. On the other hand, there is a clear imperative that governments commit their most ardent energies and resources to the welfare of the people, more than anything else.

In the current unprecedented environment of international relations with the centres of economic power moving to Asia, a region that is still divided by historical animosities, territorial disputes, and ideological tensions, the perceived rise of new powers and relative decline in influence of old ones, increases the risk of strategic competition among them. The lessons of the Cold War must be remembered by ASEAN and India: bipolar conflict hurt the interests of those who are not the major parties but are forced to take sides (including India

> "*Both ASEAN and India can benefit most from a multipolar balance and peaceful coexistence among diverse countries, big or small, in the region and the world, even as peaceful economic and technological competition takes place.*"

and ASEAN), distracting us from the all-important business of social and economic development as well as political integration and nation-building. The lessons of the immediate post-Cold War period must also be recalled: a unipolar world is undesirable and unacceptable; it stands against international norms and lacks legitimacy.

What we see now is the growing trend of multipolarity. Both ASEAN and India can benefit most from a multipolar balance and peaceful coexistence among diverse countries, big or small, in the region and the world, even as peaceful economic and technological competition takes place. Peaceful coexistence should not be a passive concept as in the past, based only on non-interference in internal affairs or a "live and let live" approach. It should be a pro-active effort based on respect for our diversity but focusing on shared interests, common aspirations, and parallel challenges facing our countries and peoples.

> "*ASEAN and India have a shared maritime environment, particularly where the Indian Ocean meets the South China Sea, in the Straits of Malacca and Singapore, and in Indonesia's westernmost waters.*"

Cooperation to address non-traditional security problems precisely emphasizes shared interests, common aspirations and parallel challenges. The non-traditional challenges to security transcend security of the state and survival of incumbent regimes and ruling parties. They may encompass the security as well as welfare of entire populations, communities, business enterprises, or individuals, not only within national boundaries but transnationally and even across the planet. Climate change, energy supply shortfalls, pandemics, natural disasters, large-scale environmental and food crises, human trafficking, trafficking in illegal substances, cybercrime, high seas piracy, and other threats to economic activity and people's livelihood are key examples of these. Unlike conventional security challenges, the solutions lie not in competitive arms build-up or zero-sum politics of power but in our ability to share information, undertake coordinated actions, strengthen and reinforce each other's capability, agree on goals and targets as well as appropriate means, and most important and difficult of all, prioritize long-term collective good over short-term interests of any single one.

Maritime Security

One such area for non-traditional security cooperation between ASEAN and India is in maritime security, where coordination is being pursued and may further be developed on several fronts. ASEAN and India have a shared maritime environment, particularly where the Indian Ocean meets the South China Sea, in the Straits of Malacca and Singapore, and in Indonesia's westernmost waters. Much of energy imports of China, Japan, South Korea and Taiwan travel from the Middle East through the Indian Ocean before transacting these narrow passages, as do a lot of other commodities traded by the United States and East Asia. The freedom and safety of shipping in the Indian Ocean and in the South China Sea (against piracy, against potential terrorist attack, against states that may impede navigation for other reasons) are fundamental to energy supply and to the open international commerce that we all value in this region, and on which the success of the global economy relies.

As ASEAN-India trade increases, the security of sealanes (apart from land interconnectivities) will become even more critical to both sides for its own sake and not just because of East Asia and Pacific-bound trade and energy flows. If in the past and until twenty years ago, ASEAN and India chose to ignore each other and concentrated instead on their respective sub-regional spheres of interest, in the future increasing trade and people-to-people flows will make sealane security as well as freedom of navigation a vital shared interest.

> "*Cooperation should be much easier to pursue between India and ASEAN than between ASEAN and certain other major powers (and as a matter of fact, even easier than among certain ASEAN states themselves, who still lack the political will to set aside some border and territorial disputes with each other).*"

As already noted by many, India and ASEAN do not have any territorial or maritime boundary disputes among themselves. Cooperation should be much easier to pursue between India and ASEAN than between ASEAN and certain other major powers (and as a matter of fact, even easier than among certain ASEAN states themselves, which still lack the political will to set aside some border and territorial disputes with each other). Information sharing and coordination of responses to such threats as piracy, maritime terrorism, and possibly other illegal and dangerous uses of the ocean, can be further pursued particularly between India and the three ASEAN states on the Malacca Straits – Indonesia, Malaysia and Singapore. Some ASEAN countries and India are part of multilateral arrangements such as the Japan-supported ReCAAP and the Information Fusion Center in Singapore, which tracks the movements of tens of thousands of ships worldwide. India already has bilateral arrangements with the United States to assist in escorting some of its high-value ships through the Malacca Straits. Smaller "mini-laterals" and bilaterals with relevant ASEAN countries could perhaps help strengthen such efforts, also to help prepare for the time when it may become necessary for regional states to go beyond monitoring and information sharing.

There are already many proposals for maritime security cooperation between India and ASEAN, addressing a range of issues pertaining to good order at sea, specifically smuggling, human trafficking, environmental threats, disaster response, etc., mainly in the nature of (1) sharing of information and experiences; (2) establishment of coordination mechanisms; (3) sharing of technologies; and (4) assistance in building capacities of individual states to enforce measures within areas of national jurisdiction. China and ASEAN have also been pursuing maritime security cooperation on their agenda of cooperation and at some point, it would be interesting and important to bring the initiatives together. The participants are not necessarily navies but various civilian agencies tasked with law enforcement – coast guards, shipping authorities, fisheries agencies, etc.

Global Commons

Is it a double-edged sword, a discourse that undermines UNCLOS at a time when most states in Southeast Asia, China are trying to comply with UNCLOS?

In SCS, there may be very little area that can be technically treated as international waters or global commons as much of seas are within the 200-nm EEZ limits or 350-nm extended continental shelf limits of littoral states and therefore subject to national jurisdiction of one type or another. This explains the sensitivity of coastal states to questions of sovereignty, and perceived challenges to their jurisdiction rights. There are differences in interpretation of certain provisions in the Law of the Seas, and perhaps, no incentive to open up discussions for as long as US, a primary user of the ocean, continues to be outside the treaty.

Maritime security cooperation must develop as a subset of the broader question of ocean governance. In Southeast Asia, the realization of the need for maritime security cooperation and ocean governance will continue to be confounded by territorial and maritime boundary disputes, and the lack of trust between states with unequal power attributes. Thus, efforts to build an inclusive, multilateral maritime security regime must go hand in hand with confidence-building measures, serious commitment to try to resolve boundary delimitation issues among regional states, and consultations leading to agreement on interpretation of LOS provisions, without which there will be no legal and normative framework upon which to proceed.

There are many challenges ahead, the vision of cooperation is clearer than the manner by which we should go about attaining it. That is precisely why we need to sustain the dialogue.

Shri Amar Nath Ram

Former Secretary, Ministry of External Affairs, India

Perhaps, it is a truism to suggest that the geo-strategic landscape in the Asia Pacific is undergoing significant changes. While the threats, not causes, of military conflicts have receded, new security threats of non-traditional dimensions seem to be growing and posing new challenges to the region and beyond. While some of these threats have their origins in domestic socio-economic causes, most can be said to have external dimensions. For example, terrorism, extremism, transnational crime and its nexus with drugs, narcotics, money-laundering, trafficking in arms and humans, piracy, maritime security and proliferation of weapons of mass destruction are examples of the external dimensions of such non-traditional threats. If we add to this natural disasters, pandemics, environmental degradation, climate change, etc., the challenges multiply.

The ARF-ASEAN discourse on this subject, at present, mostly seems to focus on traditional conflict prevention, preventive diplomacy, and confidence-building measures leading to conflict resolution. This continues to be the underlying theme in the ARF vision statement and the other related documents with non-traditional threats receiving a somewhat lower attention.

As far as India and ASEAN are concerned, trade and economics alone cannot any longer drive or determine the changing nature or contour of this important relationship. India and ASEAN and a number of other countries of the region are now strategic partners engaged in annual summit level dialogues. They need to examine some of these questions in greater depth. Therefore, the scope and nature of our strategic dialogue now needs to be expanded and deepened to reflect the imperatives of today. Moving forward from the traditional and limited focus of our dialogue, we now need to discuss and coalesce our respective positions on a variety of important issues of contemporary concern especially existing and emerging non-traditional threats to security, transnational crime and the other challenges mentioned earlier.

"*Moving forward from the traditional and limited focus of our dialogue, we now need to discuss and coalesce our respective positions on a variety of important issues of contemporary concern especially existing and emerging non-traditional threats to security, transnational crime and the other challenges.*"

The emergence of China as a player in the strategically important region has implications which have been alluded to. At the same time, the emergence of India and its potential is happily seen as a positive and benign factor in the Asia Pacific.

A discussion on the future role of the ARF is already under way in the ARF and its affiliate bodies. Arguably it needs to be made more proactive and action oriented. Its scope and structure needs to be reordered to reflect today's concerns. Its recommendatory character also needs to be reviewed and its allied bodies may need to be given sharper focus. The current ARF discourse on the subject of its own reform perhaps lacks sufficient thrust and focus, and this also perhaps needs to be factored into India-ASEAN, India-ARF dialogue in the third decade of the Look East Policy.

There have been suggestions regarding the role of the military, defence establishments in enhancing mutual confidence. Happily this

"*The current ARF discourse on the subject of its own reform perhaps lacks sufficient thrust and focus, and this also perhaps needs to be factored into India-ASEAN, India-ARF dialogue in the third decade of the Look East Policy.*"

has begun to happen. Institutionalized and structured coordination and cooperation between the military, naval and coastguard establishments under ARF aegis can become a meaningful instrument for coordinated action. The direct involvement and inputs of the military services in the ARF process could be useful. The role of the regional navies and the coastguards is crucial in ensuring and promoting maritime security, safety of the sea lanes, fight against transnational crime and piracy, checking terrorist activities, and in meeting the challenge of natural disasters like the tsunami.

One final point is that there can be no better insurance in combating non-traditional threats to security than broad-basing India-ASEAN relations through people-to-people contacts on an institutionalized basis. Suffice it to say at this point of time that the agenda for India-ASEAN, India-ARF dialogue in the third decade of our Look East Policy now needs to be made more broad-based, more meaningful, greater attention to the non-traditional threats to security and indeed in how our cooperation can enhance not only regional peace but global peace.

H.E. Mr. U Aye Lwin

Director-General (ASEAN) (retd.), Myanmar

The idea of people-to-people contact has remained confined to educated people, of course, to facilitate infrastructure development, bridge building, roads, highways and also institutional improvements, to make the flow easier of people and goods. There is a need for different types of people-to-people contact. If we look at the population of Asian countries, majority of them come from the farming communities. In other words, Asian countries are still agricultural countries. There is a need to set up a farmers' and farming communities' network if we want to connect larger number of people.

To set up farmers and farming communities' network, we would need intermediate organizations like civil society groups or NGOs. If there are enough incentives for the farmers to be in touch with each other, it would be a great thing in terms of people-to-people contacts. This suggestion is more in terms of improvement of the environment. The natural farming techniques, where the farmers are at least taught to make their own bio-fertilizers, means reduced cost of production and also a surplus amount of funds. Also most farmers are dependent in our region on microfinance, dependent on having capital to do the farming but they never manage to get out of this rut of indebtedness.

One of the ways to escape the cycle of indebtedness is to come up with practical income generation projects, such as animal breeding. However, there is nothing new about it and is already used in our part of the world. If they are taught the techniques to do it right and then to provide them the funds that they need to start the project, in time the income that is generated would be a source of extra fund to repay the loan for the normal agricultural activities.

Farmers' and farming communities' networks is an incentive for exchange of ideas on the techniques for the farmers for generation of income from the projects. This sort of thing might give incentive for the intermediary organizations, civil society groups to create enough incentives to bring the farmers in our region gradually together.

INDIA IN THE ADMM PLUS AND THE EAS PROCESS: THE NEXT DECADE

Dato' Dr. William R. Stevenson
Shri Shivshankar Menon
Mr. Samuel B. Bagasin
H.E. Mr. Pham Quang Vinh
Prof. K.S. Nathan
Mr. Sabam P. Siagian
Ms. Connie Rahakundini Bakrie

Dato' Dr. William R. Stevenson

Executive Director, Malaysian Institute of Defence and Security, Kuala Lumpur

The East Asia Summit or ASEAN plus six (namely ASEAN plus China, Japan, South Korea, India, Australia and New Zealand) and now plus eight with US and Russia, since its inception, has served as a platform for dialogue for broad strategic issues of relevance to East Asia, covering regional and global issue with the focus on areas such as terrorism, energy, infectious diseases, poverty reduction and sustainable development. The last summit was held in October 2010 in Hanoi, Vietnam and we also witnessed the inaugural ASEAN Plus Defense Ministerial Meeting or the ADMM Plus.

As we are aware the economic growth among countries of ASEAN and its neighbours has also led to growth in military spending and growth in military power among nations in the region. We dealt with "soft power" in the earlier sessions. There is also the need to look at military power and the emerging security architecture of the region.

> "*India has indeed a significant role to play for the stability of the region, especially with the other growing nations in the region, such as China.*"

The security issues in the Asia Pacific are reflected on a range of factors namely the geography of the region with its complex patterns of archipelagos, islands, bays and gulfs and narrow shipping channels, the heavy dependence on shipping for both domestic and intra regional trade and the importance of regional seas and its resources. Meanwhile with other factors including the impact of globalization, sovereignty issues, the increasing levels and density of sea, air and land traffic in the region, and with growing military budgets, we see a higher level of military activities in the region. Besides that, the involvement of non-state actors and transnational threats has added to the menaces that need equal attention from regional states. The combination and complexities of these factors impact on the challenges in promoting security in the region.

India has been having active engagements with countries in the region, whether bilaterally or multilaterally. India-ASEAN relationship has been intensified significantly in the recent years with the growing situation. India has indeed a significant role to play for the stability of the region, especially with the other growing nations in the region, such as China.

The ADMM-Plus functions as a platform for strategic dialogue and consultation with a view to build common views or perception on regional security, enhancing mutual confidence, trust and identifying areas of practical cooperation. The countries involved in the ADMM Plus also constitute the membership of the East Asia Summit (EAS) and also members of the ARF (ASEAN Regional Forum).

India has an important role to play in determining the outcome of the security in the Asia-Pacific region. Nevertheless, the driving force for cooperation and stability shall be relevant to all ADMM Plus member states and with mutual trust and confidence this framework will also be the platform for conflict resolution. We also hope that the emerging architecture and new approaches will have realistic solutions and will be of benefit to all. Of course, it should be guided by the principle of mutual understanding, concern, consultation and cooperation among the members states.

Shri Shivshankar Menon

National Security Advisor, Government of India

In 2012, we observe the twentieth anniversary of the India-ASEAN dialogue process and in the last twenty years we have given contemporary relevance to an old historic relationship. From a relatively modest start we have managed to achieve a great deal in our dialogue. We now have a multifaceted interaction whether in politics, in economics and now increasingly in security. Therefore, there is a need to speak about how we in India, at least, see the geopolitical situation around us in Asia, and what issues that throws up for us and how then we can work together and how we see both the ADMM process and the EAS as critical to the way in which we move forward on these issues.

We are in a continent, which is the fastest changing part of the world and in a region where security cooperation now is becoming increasingly crucial and critical to our futures. We see shifting balances of power in Asia. This is not just a consequence of growth. It is also the fact that this is a very crowded environment. There are several powers, developing rapidly at the same time. They are not just established powers but powers which are rising. We see them undertaking internal balancing – the sort of defence

> “*We are in a continent, which is the fastest changing part of the world and in a region where security cooperation now is becoming increasingly crucial and critical to our futures.*”

budgets that was just mentioned – as well as external balancing in terms of relationships with each other.

Secondly, this is the most rapidly changing, growing, and developing part of the world. In fact the global economic crisis seems to have actually shifted the centre of gravity even more so to our part of the world. It seems that for the foreseeable future this is where the strategic centre of gravity will be, and where we will have to deal with the security issues.

Thirdly, as the fastest growing, developing part of the world, we also have the most to lose from instability and insecurity in the international system. We do not often quite realize this. But we have the most at stake in maintaining in the foreseeable future the present trajectory. And we have a stake in preventing the kind of instability and insecurity which could affect us, which could affect our future growth. Since the way in which we have grown is really by our own horizontal integration of capital, of goods, of services, markets both across the region and into global chains, since that is they way we have grown, it therefore becomes even more important that we be able to secure our links with each other and with the rest of the world.

It logically follows from the pattern of growth, from the way in which we have developed, that the number one security issue is being able to secure our own communications among ourselves and with the rest of the world on which our growth, our development is dependent. In other words, maritime security and other communications links, terrorism, which can bring the kind of instability that can affect our own future development, and our cooperation in disaster relief become very important in order to develop the habits of working in these areas. And frankly if we look at our experience, we have a good record. If we look at our success in dealing with piracy around the Straits of Malacca, in the larger sense in the

> *"Maritime security and other communications links, terrorism, which can bring the kind of instability that can affect our own future development, and our cooperation in disaster relief become very important in order to develop the habits of working in these areas."*

ASEAN and the neighbouring countries, we can claim to have been among the most successful examples. On the other hand, we have not been so successful in the Horn of Africa. That was because we evolved structures and ways of working together, on our own without any ideology, without too much fuss. That is a very useful experience to have and it gives the confidence that while going ahead we will be able to deal with the security issues that we face.

> *"From an Indian point of view, Asian Security Architecture should be open, flexible and inclusive. And it must include all the relevant powers whether they are of the region itself or even extrinsic but are relevant in practice and have presence in the region. It should also be plural."*

What sort of Asian order would deal with these issues? One can argue logically. Do we do what we did in the economic field? Do we do building block upon building block, sort of feeling our way forward slowly, much of it informal which we then formalize? Or do we try some big grand structure of collective security? It has been tried before in the Cold War. Both the superpowers tried to organize us all around these principles. It did not work. The Asian way is the best that we do exactly as we did when we dealt with piracy. When we faced a concrete issue, we learnt how to deal with it and we did it ourselves. And there are no answers to these questions of how is the best way forward. That is something we have to work out together.

What is desirable from Asian security architecture? From an Indian point of view, it should be open, it should be flexible and it should be inclusive. It has to be inclusive because given the diversity in Asia, both in terms of power and in terms of the interest, it is essential if the order is to work. And it must include all the relevant powers whether they are of the region itself or even extrinsic but are relevant in practice and have presence in the region. It should also be plural. Our entire experience suggests that no one size fits all. We will deal with the kinds of issues, just listed above.

And it should respect our Asian cultural bias towards consensual solutions.

Therefore, we warmly welcome and actually strongly encourage the ADMM Plus process and the EAS because they meet all the criteria which we think logically follow from our situation for a nation's security order. We are ready to do whatever we can to strengthen both these processes, which are, from our point of view, logical and practical. ASEAN, therefore, is central to our conception of the future of Asian security.

Our own experience and expertize will be made available to our partners as we work our way forward. And this sharp focus on concrete confidence-building measures through cooperation in specific areas of common interest is the right way forward. This architecture offers us the potential also of creating coherent, concerted responses to the kinds of threats mentioned, whether it is on maritime security or on the others.

We see the EAS, which, let us not forget, is relatively new – five years is not that long in the life of an organization – as providing the overarching framework within which we can actually carry on this work. We are confident that both of them will contribute meaningfully to enhancing stability, security and ultimately mutual prosperity within the region.

Mr. Samuel B. Bagasin

Under Secretary, Department of Defence, the Philippines

The Philippines welcomes India's participation in the recently established ASEAN Plus Defence Ministers Meeting. The Philippines regards India as an important stakeholder in the Asia-Pacific security architecture. It has given valuable contributions in various conferences and dialogues especially in the East Asia Summit. We see India's inclusion in the ADMM Plus as a continued strengthening of its role in promoting regional peace and stability.

> *"The Philippines regards India as an important stakeholder in the Asia-Pacific security architecture."*

India became one of the first members of the EAS since its establishment in 2005. India's relations with China and other emerging countries as well as with the ASEAN member states have been a stabilizing force in the community-building initiatives in the region. India has led the cooperative activities under the EAS in trade and economy such as being one of the lead countries in the topical study on a comprehensive economic partnership in East Asia. This is to further develop the East Asia free trade area.

At the same time, India as a key partner in promoting ASEAN regional integration remains committed to the realization of the ASEAN community through promoting efforts and initiatives such as the ASEAN Plus free trade areas. India has also forged cultural, and defence links with the EAS and the ASEAN member countries which reinforces the momentum for community-building. Moreover, considering the close and productive relations with both the ASEAN and the emerging powers, India's participation in the ADMM Plus ensures that the ADMM Plus initiatives would be undertaken at a pace comfortable to all members.

This economic and strategic strength of India underscore its important role in promoting peace, security and stability in the region as well as strengthening cooperation, strategic, political, and economic issues of common interest. This demonstrates India's stand in upholding global norms and values that will help in advancing international peace and equitable development in the region. From the various initiatives that India has launched in the areas of counterterrorism, maritime security, peacekeeping operations, and humanitarian assistance and disaster response in recent years, we see India's commitment and valuable role in strengthening these initiatives through its participation in the Experts Working Groups or the EWGs in the ADMM Plus.

"*Considering that the Indian armed forces have been known for its excellent service in various peacekeeping missions in the world, the Philippines as the ASEAN co-chair of the Experts Working Group on peacekeeping operations is very keen on working particularly with India in enhancing ADMM Plus member states' peacekeeping capabilities.*"

Further, considering that the Indian armed forces have been known for its excellent service in various peacekeeping missions in the world, the Philippines as the ASEAN co-chair of the Experts Working Group on peacekeeping operations is very keen on working particularly with India in enhancing ADMM Plus member states' peacekeeping capabilities. We would also like to explore the possibility of having regional arrangements for peacekeeping operations in the world. The Philippines looks forward to working with India at both the bilateral level as well as a member of the ASEAN and within these frameworks.

H.E. Mr. Pham Quang Vinh

Assistant Minister for Foreign Affairs, Vietnam

Last year, we in ASEAN and East Asia made two important decisions. One is to convene the first and inaugural ADMM Plus and we decided to expand EAS to include two other major powers the USA and Russia. A lot of implications and a lot of intentions that we in ASEAN and together with dialogue partners in East Asia have put into that decision-making. We conceived ADMM Plus and the expanding EAS as integral parts of the emerging regional architecture in this region. Another part is that as we have the new ADMM Plus and the newly expanded EAS, they did not have specific and respective roles but complement to each other within the context of the regional architecture that we are developing. Hence, with regard to regional architecture, suddenly, there have been efforts to try to define and to put forward a kind of regional architecture that is good for the region for stability, for security, for peace and cooperation including economic integration. ASEAN has been at the centre of all these efforts.

Over the years, ASEAN has been continuing its efforts for regional integration including ASEAN community building. ASEAN has developed an initiative and developed a network of regional processes such as ASEAN+1, ASEAN+3, EAS, ARF, etc. All these have been serving well throughout the years. But there are also ideas of how we will develop an overall mechanism for this vision. There have been different proposals for that. We can say that the decision of this region last year to have the expanded EAS and also to have the ADMM plus, is a way to define the emerging regional architecture with the concurrence of the dialogue partners in this region of East Asia.

> *We need India to join ASEAN to work together in all these areas especially in defining the emerging regional architecture, the future role of the expanded EAS and enhancing the good start of the ADMM Plus.*

For ASEAN, we should base ourselves on the existing regional processes and build up on it to make the regional architecture. The different processes will have different roles but they can have some overlapping roles. They are complementary to each other and helping each other towards the common goals of peace, stability and cooperation in the region.

Another idea that ASEAN is strongly putting forward is that it should continue to maintain a central role in all these efforts and processes. We have been receiving strong support from our dialogue partners in East Asia. The reason for ASEAN's central role has been explained a lot in the past. We need to create a level-playing environment, and conducive environment for constructive contributions by the countries in the region and by the major powers that we engage.

Another point is ASEAN's forward looking nature that we are to engage the dialogue partners and the major powers in a number of ways. We need them and they need ASEAN. We need the major powers and the dialogue partners to support ASEAN in its regional efforts especially in its community building and regional integration. We need to work with the dialogue partners for the cooperation on all areas including regional economic integration. We need to work together with the dialogue partners and the major powers so that we are able to better deal and resolve the challenges that are commonly faced by the region. We appreciate the constructive roles to be played by the major powers and the dialogue partners including the USA and Russia. But when they are in this region, we need the major powers to support ASEAN's central role in all these efforts and at the same time, work together among themselves constructively also.

Within this regional architecture, ADMM Plus and the expanded EAS will be important. Though we will have a new EAS with its new members, the principles, modalities and objectives of the grouping remain the same. The EAS will continue to be the leaders' forum for dialogue and cooperation on strategic issues including in economic areas, in political and security areas. Russia and the USA will certainly focus more on political and security issues. The challenge is how to balance this and continue with our ongoing efforts that we have achieved so far, in the last five years, including the initiative on Comprehensive Economic Partnership in East Asia (CEPEA) or on the five priorities that we have set for the EAS. That is one thing that we need to discuss further.

Since we are engaging the US and Russia, which are major powers, it is important to maintain the driving role and the centrality of ASEAN. It is also important to discuss how India is going to continue to play a prominent role in the EAS. And, if we are to discuss more often political and security issues, what will be the modalities for discussing these issues and measures that we can comfortably take towards cooperation? Moreover, the five priority areas that include economic and other fields, are not quite political and security issues.

And for the ADMM Plus, five Working Groups have identified the areas that we need to focus our cooperation on – on maritime security, on peace-keeping, on counterterrorism, on military, and disaster and humanitarian assistance. We have already been working on these areas in this region. The new thing is that the defence channel at the highest level between ASEAN and the eight dialogue partners will work together in this field. This framework will continue to build confidence and enhance our cooperation.

These forums can also contribute to the cooperation over non-traditional security issues – maritime security including maritime security in the South China Sea for example, counterterrorism, disaster management, and piracy. Today, we have new mechanisms, dialogue partners and new format of cooperation. The 17th ARF meeting discussed the South China Sea issue, which has three important aspects. The first aspect is peace and security including maritime security that is very important for this region and we should work together through various forums to achieve and maintain that. There is a declaration on the conduct of the parties concerned on the South China Sea and ASEAN and China should work together harder to ensure its full and effective implementation in order to create an environment of confidence, stability and security. Specific territorial claims or overlapping claims have to be resolved by the parties concerned and the resolution must reflect the spirit of the DOC.

Since all the three forums – the ADMM Plus, expanded EAS and the ARF – touch upon the question of political and security in the region, there is a need to coordinate our activities in these forums and make their roles not competing with each other but complementary and supporting each other.

We need India to join ASEAN to work together in all these areas especially in defining the emerging regional architecture, the future role of the expanded EAS and enhancing the good start of the ADMM Plus.

Prof. K.S. Nathan

Director, Institute of Malaysian and International Studies, IKMAS

This region is characterized by changing strategic dynamics resulting from the increasing pace of globalization but with the proviso that the nation state continues to be very resilient. In fact, it is the strength of the nation state and its ability to survive all kinds of challenges that have also enabled cooperation on so many fronts, and institutionalization of the security architecture in the region. It is interesting that despite many challenges of globalization, the most resilient animal has been the nation state. The second point is the growing international capacity of formerly dormant powers, China and India. The third point is the consolidation of regional security processes and institutions such as the ASEAN community, the ARF, the East Asia Summit process, the ADMM and of course now the ADMM Plus. Yet, it is important to also note that there is continuity in maintaining a general framework of Asia-Pacific stability via the US's strategic presence, the US-Japan alliance and other US led bilateral and multilateral security arrangements.

> *"The EAS process is not based on tight institutionalization, a very important fact about the Asian strategic culture. We can live with a lot of ambiguity and perhaps that is our strength because we can seek clarity in ambiguity."*

Amidst all these changes, there is still an element of continuing strategic stability provided by the US security cover which nobody has really questioned. Even cold-warriors who were opposed to the United

States now see that there is value in America providing that cover simply because it is too expensive for anyone to take on the US role and provide the same strategic presence for the entire Asia-Pacific. It is better to piggyback on security provided by somebody which has now become a common good.

It is interesting to look at the concept of the EAS and how Asian security is being structured. The political economy of the region is undergoing a major transformation. There are new players and these new players are principally China and India which are now taking a greater portion of Asian trade and obviously, and concomitantly, the US share is declining. This means, politics, economics and security are even more closely linked with all actors having a direct interest in the stability and security of the region to continue harvesting the "Post Cold War dividend." The economic integration between Northeast and Southeast Asia is stronger than economic integration within Northeast Asian countries. And that is because of the persistence of Cold War mentalities in the region. The Cold War is not over for China and Korea as we know. China is divided between China and Taiwan and of course Korea is still divided, North Korea and South Korea, along the thirty-eighth Parallel. Hence, integration is weaker there.

The EAS process is not based on tight institutionalization, a very important fact about the Asian strategic culture. We can live with a lot of ambiguity and perhaps that is our strength because we can seek clarity in ambiguity. There are several issues that still remain unresolved which need to be tackled. This is part of the Asian strategic scenario. The China-Taiwan issue, the North Korea-South Korea issue, the nuclear threat posed by Pyongyang, and of course irritants in the Japan-China political relations as well.

The inclusion of the Plus 3 into ASEAN Plus 3 that is ASEAN Plus China, Japan and South Korea, and plus India, Australia and New Zealand, is a recognition that inclusivity would yield better results than exclusivity based on questionable racial or geographical criteria. The main point about economics is that we want people to sit around the table who can contribute. There is no point in having actors around the table who have nothing to bring to the table. So, geography has become irrelevant. Whoever can contribute, welcome them and see how we can use their strengths to synergize further.

Australia has always been trying to claim or trying to get entry as an Asian nation. The question is why should Australia want to be an Asian nation? Australia should be Australia. And we deal with Australia on the basis of what Australia can give us and what Australia can take from the region. There is no need to change the identity. Geography and geographical criteria have been irrelevant. What is relevant is the strength that each can bring to a particular situation. That is why the EAS has expanded in so many ways to become even more inclusive because every member has something to contribute and also to take from the forum.

> *"Cooperative security is going to be the currency of the future in Southeast Asia and also the broader Asia, encompassing, therefore, concepts of ADMM Plus and EAS."*

The rise of India, of course, is as much a fact as the rise of China in 1990s. Now both are becoming major centres of production, investment and trade for the whole world including ASEAN's major dialogue partners. Washington feels more comfortable with EAS through the inclusion of, what it considers to be, its friends and allies in the current political equilibrium. They are India, Australia and New Zealand. These three countries have strong ties with Southeast Asia based on a combination of one or more elements – history, culture, trade, commerce, investment, and security.

The EAS process provides yet another forum for member countries to discuss strategies to maintain and expand the concept of open regionalism. Again, this is a major driver of regional integration, something very peculiar to our region. ASEAN practices open regionalism, a major driver that embraces the notion of inclusivity and more importantly cooperative security. This is an important concept in the Post Cold War era because cooperative security is a non-threat based conception. We do not identify anybody as a threat. Everyone is seen as a friend and an ally in the common endeavour. That is why co-operative security is going to be the currency of the future in Southeast Asia and also the broader Asia, encompassing therefore concepts of ADMM Plus and EAS. The ADMM Plus concept and framework pointedly indicates that threat perceptions and projections are becoming less important while potential for cooperation is being steadily explored including in defence and security matters.

Looking ahead, we can see further intensification and institutionalization of political, economic and security process with ADMM Plus playing a key role in many areas of non-traditional security, such as peacekeeping operations, pandemics, humanitarian assistance, disaster relief, and of course combating piracy and also international terrorism. The ADMM Plus is yet another mechanism that complements rather than conflicts with existing regional processes such as the ASEAN Regional Forum, as well as bilateral and multi-lateral security arrangements largely led by the United States.

Nevertheless, there are major challenges on this highway towards a further, fuller, and more comprehensive engagement. What is the challenge for ASEAN where it relates to the India-ASEAN nexus? The challenge is in developing a deeper knowledge, understanding and appreciation of how India ticks in order to optimize and maximize the synergies that arise. And what is the challenge for India, the big challenge? Is there a unity of perception and purpose on foreign policy, regional security and integration held by the Foreign Ministry, Defence Ministry, Economic Ministry and also the bureaucracy. Since India is a multinational nation, the inherent complexities of managing the world's largest and most populous democracy would necessarily include containing the tendency towards insularity and encouraging the more desirable and perhaps inevitable trend towards universality.

Mr. Sabam P. Siagian
Director and Senior Editor, Jakarta Post, Indonesia

The overall theme of the conference – beyond the first twenty years of India and East Asia engagement – and the particular theme of our session means that for years to come, we are facing a changing geopolitical map, especially with the rise of China and India. However, the two countries from the outset are not already in a confrontational trajectory. But as Robert D. Kaplan points out in an article in Foreign Affairs in 2009 and expanded that in his recent remarkable book, *Monsoon: Indian Ocean and the Future American Power*, that both rising countries India and China, especially China have to secure their long supply lines. High economic growth means higher import of energy and mining minerals. As Hu Jintao said, the Strait of Malacca is our dilemma. Eighty-five per cent of China's import of energy products goes through the Strait of Malacca. And that means an increased joint responsibility of Malaysia, Indonesia, Singapore and other ASEAN countries.

India, in an indirect way, is fighting the feuds of us friends. First of all, India should enhance its diplomatic presence in the East Asia countries by beefing up its embassies with quality staffing and adequate operational funds. The activities related to the public

> "*India should enhance its diplomatic presence in the East Asia countries by beefing up its embassies with quality staffing and adequate operational funds. The activities related to the public diplomacy should be expanded.*"

diplomacy should be expanded. In all these countries in ASEAN and in East Asia, there have been sociological changes. New actors are popping up. The government has a diminishing role day by day. So, the activities related to the public diplomacy should be expanded including spreading the rich Indian culture also in its modern forms. The magic world of Bollywood is India's effective communication channel.

The Indian Navy should increase its activities in East Asia by frequent port calls and various joint naval exercises. Whatever joint programmes of ADMM Plus are planning, India should offer its active participation. The Indian Naval Chief Admiral Arun Prakash made a port call to Jakarta in July 2005 with a squadron of the Carrier INS Virat accompanied by two guided missile destroyers. This type of frequent appearance of Indian naval officers in port calls in East Asia would enhance India's engagement with the emerging pattern in East Asia.

Even though connectivity is being talked about and Myanmar is understood as the land bridge between India and ASEAN, the real connectivity with Myanmar still has to be established. India has an important role to play because of its size and its historical background to help the majority of ASEAN members in persuading the leadership in Myanmar towards human rights and democracy in Myanmar. The competition for energy sources in Myanmar with China should not diminish India's keenness in nudging Myanmar to accept democracy and human rights. If, even after thirty years, the situation is more or less remains the same, ASEAN does not deserve to be praised by the rest of the world.

"The Indian Navy should increase its activities in East Asia by frequent port calls and various joint naval exercises. Whatever joint programmes of ADMM Plus are planning, India should offer its active participation."

Ms. Connie Rahakundini Bakrie

Lecturer, University of Indonesia

Any discussion over the concepts of defence and security raises the questions of defence and security for whom, of which values, from what threats and challenges, and defence and security by what means. Any such security perspective is complicated.

The powerful engine of growth actually lies in these waters. Seventy per cent of the surface is covered by waters and the seas are linked with each other. Eighty per cent of life on this planet lives in the water as well. To take full advantage of the geographical contiguity of Southeast Asia and India and the synergized strength of the two significant economic regions, the sea has become the engine of growth. Indonesia is between the Indian Ocean and the Malay Pacific and its geographic location highlights the importance of the country.

Jakarta needs to find a balance between the economic and security aspects of its foreign policy. Probably the security is a complex matter. First, it depends on the location that can be identified at regional, sub-regional or cross-regional levels. Second, it depends on the density of relationships – how thick or thin are the ties. Finally, it depends on the identification of interests – for whose interest. The security of ASEAN is still an under-developed concept. ASEAN's security co-

> “*India can play an important role in protecting our marine resources and maritime biodiversity.*”

operation is based only on dialogue and consensus and avoiding problems instead of resolving them.

The security of ASEAN should be focused on its maritime aspects. As Robert Kaplan said, no Ocean is in need of strategic stability more than the Indian Ocean today. Indonesia is at the centre of ASEAN and critical hub of ASEAN. Maritime security cannot be entirely left to Indonesia, to the ASEAN or other regional bodies. Rather, it has to be a collective maritime security.

Indonesia is located in a region that is becoming an arena of the big power struggle. The question facing Indonesia is how to build a maritime security alliance. One of the biggest threats facing our region is the private military companies. The private military companies, protecting ships or vessels are dangerous and it has become a very big business. The private military companies are running this kind of business in our waters – protection of ports, underwater assets, offshore energy installations, energy supply chains, fishing grounds, large fishing boats, cruise ships, navy vessels visiting foreign ports. When they feel insecure they invite the private military, and even the crisis management. This can make the narrow Strait of Malacca a dangerous strait. If one ship is just stuck over there, all the movement of goods will be stopped.

Indonesia's military strength is limited. Only 52 per cent of its warships, 56 per cent of the marine combat strength and 45 per cent of its air force are actually functional. Maybe we believe in ASEAN way and believe that everything would be solved peacefully. We have to work with India, which is increasing its defence budget. India can play an important role in protecting our marine resources and maritime biodiversity.

CONCLUDING REMARKS

Shri Sudhir T. Devare

Shri Sudhir T. Devare

Director-General, Indian Council of World Affairs, New Delhi

Delhi Dialogue is a new process and will, in the future, combine a holistic and comprehensive dialogue. ASEAN and India is now a new engine, a formidable force in the Asia-Pacific region. It was described as an arc of opportunity, located on a transmission belt of economic, prosperity, stability and security.

There are two-three issues on which India and ASEAN must, in the coming months, work hard and conclude the pending agreements. One was the Comprehensive Economic Cooperation Agreement on which only trade in goods has been signed so far and negotiations on services and investment are still continuing.

There was broad agreement that connectivity between India and ASEAN in every respect must be developed and that included physical connectivity of roads, railways, air traffic, shipping and so on but also institutional capacity, cyber connectivity and indeed connectivity between the people. The people-to-people exchanges and communications were emphasized time and again.

We also looked towards 2012 and beyond. The year of 2012 will mark the twentieth anniversary of the commencement of the India-ASEAN dialogue which began with the sectoral dialogue in 1992. It also marks the tenth anniversary of the India-ASEAN Summit. The leaders have already agreed to have a commemorative summit in Delhi and the Indian Prime Minister has invited all ASEAN Heads of State and Government to come to Delhi for this Summit.

We should be now preparing for this major event next year and in that context we had a preliminary exchange of views on what should be really going into this summit. There were a number of thoughts which were expressed. It was felt that there are new issues which have come up; there are new challenges which have come up; challenges of food security, energy security, those which we had not really applied ourselves to so far all these years. Unless we succeed in tackling these issues, India and ASEAN will not have very durable relationship.

There was a suggestion that India should enhance its naval presence in South China Sea. Some new ideas were expressed. It was stated that there should be greater military exchanges between India and ASEAN.

On connectivity, a number of new ideas were stated and it was felt that India and ASEAN should take every possible step to bridge this gap which has existed all these years between India and ASEAN.

> "*It would be useful to really coordinate between ASEAN and India to work out some kind of an informal agenda for EAS*"

On the non-traditional security issues, which have continued to dominate the discourse between ASEAN and India over the years even in the ASEAN Regional Forum and other fora, we have mainly tackled these issues. There again we felt that there are new issues like climate change which can have wide ramifications across ASEAN and India. It was, at the same time, pointed out that while we may be exposed to risks, it does not mean that the vulnerabilities have increased. In fact, we should be taking steps to mitigate those vulnerabilities. India and ASEAN should come up with a concrete action plan.

Indeed, before we go to EAS late this year, it would be useful to really coordinate between ASEAN and India to work out some kind of an informal agenda for EAS because it was pointed out that with the United States and Russia joining in the EAS, we must deliver. That stands true for ASEAN as well as for India. ASEAN is certainly at the core of EAS, it is the fulcrum around which EAS as indeed other ASEAN institutions function. Unless ASEAN countries and India are seen to be really bringing something very concrete in these processes, the credibility of these institutions will progressively go down. Therefore, the responsibility for this action rests both with India as well as ASEAN.

From this point of view, a suggestion was made that India should add its voice to that of ASEAN so as to lend greater credibility to the ASEAN proposals on non-traditional security areas at the EAS. It is really worthy of merit and deserves our attention. We should try to constitute some kind of an informal group which can go into this process well before the meeting of the EAS.

Finally, on the session on EAS process and ADMM Plus, India has welcomed its membership of EAS in 2005 and also of the ADMM Plus. In this regard, one should welcome the change of perception that one can see in ASEAN countries. Someone mentioned that Indian Navy should visit ASEAN ports more often. It reminds us of 1988-9 when Indian Naval ships were in fact almost forbidden from going to these ports because the Indian threat perception was highlighted in the international media. Indian Navy was regarded as a major threatening force. Over the last twenty years, much water has flowed down the Malacca Straits. This is a very happy and positive development and both of us need to build on this.

This Dialogue has been a very positive and a constructive work in progress for all of us. We need to build on this in the coming months and years.

Notes on Contributors

Aileen San Pablo-Baviera

Professor Aileen San Pablo-Baviera is currently Professor of Asian Studies at the Asian Center, University of the Philippines, where she has been teaching since 1998 and where she served as Dean during 2003-09. Her research interests include Contemporary China, International Relations, Asia-Pacific Security, and Asian Civil Society. She has edited and co-edited 11 books and monographs, and authored 5 books and monographs, 21 book chapters and 7 journal articles. Dr. Baviera lectures regularly at the Foreign Service Institute and the National Defense College of the Philippines. Overseas, she has lectured at various institutions in Japan, China, Taiwan, Malaysia and India and held research fellowships at the Japan Institute of International Affairs, Beijing University, Shanghai Institute of International Studies, Xiamen University, National Chengchi University, and joint appointment at the Institute of Malaysian and International Studies of Universiti Kebangsaan Malaysia and the Universiti Pertahanan Nasional Malaysia.

Amar Nath Ram

Shri Amar Nath Ram served for nearly 36 years in the Indian Foreign Service before retiring as Secretary in the Ministry of External Affairs, Government of India. He served as Ambassador of India to the European Union, ESCAP, Zambia, Thailand, Argentina, Bhutan, Belgium, Deputy Chief of Mission in the US and in various capacities in the Ministries of External Affairs and Commerce. He was closely associated with the Look East Policy in its initial phase and with immediate post-reform economic diplomacy. Earlier for his work in Bhutan he was awarded the country's one of the highest civilian decorations by the Royal Government of Bhutan. He continues to be closely involved at the Track II level with the Look East Policy, SAARC, South and Southeast Asian affairs. He is a member of the ASEAN Regional Forum's group of eminent persons and experts and of the India Committee of the Council for Security Cooperation in Asia-Pacific (CSCAP). He has written and published extensively. Shri A.N. Ram comments regularly in the media and writes on international issues.

Amit Mitra

Shri Amit Mitra is the Secretary-General of the Federation of Indian Chambers of Commerce and Industry (FICCI). He is also a recipient of India's prestigious "Padma Shree" award in 2008 and the recipient of highest civilian awards conferred by His Majesty, the Emperor of Japan in 2006, and President of the Republic of Italy in 2005 and 2007.

Shri Mitra is Chairman of the Expert Committee of the Indian Railways on innovative financing and has served as member on several Indian and international boards, expert groups, and committees such as the Advisory Board of the India Fund of the Unit Trust of India (UTI), Advisory Board of Microsoft Corporation (India) Pvt. Ltd., the "Eminent Persons Group" of the UNCTAD on Non-Tariff Barriers (NTBs), Expert Committee to formulate energy Policy by Planning Commission (2005-06), and the India-China Eminent Persons Group.

He is also a Member of the Joint Study Groups set up between the Governments of India-China, India-Japan, India-Israel, India-Korea & India-Russia. Mr. Mitra has authored several academic and policy writings as well as several articles in the leading Indian newspapers.

Anand Sharma

Shri Anand Sharma is currently the Minister of Commerce and Industry, Government of India. He has been a prominent public face of the Indian National Congress and was Chief Spokesman of the party for six years. He was elevated to the Union Council of Ministers with responsibility for Foreign Affairs in January 2006. He also assumed the additional charge of Union Minister of State for Information & Broadcasting in October 2008.

As Commerce and Industry Minister he re-energized the stalled Doha round talks by convening a Ministerial meeting in Delhi. The India-

ASEAN agreement and the India-Korea CECA were also signed during his tenure.

Shri Sharma has been conferred with "The Order of the Companion of Volta", top Ghanaian civilian award by President J.A. Koufour in 2008 in recognition of his commitment to South-South Cooperation. He was also honoured with the "Commander of the National Order of Merit", highest civilian award by the President of Ivory Coast on 14 January 2009.

U Aye Lwin

H.E. Mr. U Aye Lwin served in the Myanmar Foreign Service for 41 years before retiring in 2001 as the Director-General, Department of ASEAN Affairs. He served at the Permanent Mission of Myanmar to the United Nations (1963-67), and the diplomatic missions in Dhaka (1974-80) and Washington D.C. (1985-88).

H.E. Mr. U Aye Lwin served in the Ministry of Foreign Affairs, Yangon, as Director, International Law and Treaties Division (1980 to 1985); Director-General, International Organization and Economic Department (1988-89); and Director-General, Department of Consular, International Law and Treaties and Research.

H.E. Mr. U Aye Lwin participated in the United Nations General Assembly sessions (1989-93); United Nations Conference on the Law of the Sea, (UNCLOS-III) in 1981; the Preparatory Commission for the International Sea-Bed Authority; and The International Tribunal for the Law of the Sea, Kingston, Jamaica several times. H.E. Mr. U Aye Lwin spent two years as a student in St. Joseph's College, North Point, Darjeeling, India (1950-52).

C.P. Joshi

Dr. C.P. Joshi is currently the Minister of Road Transport and Highways, Government of India. He previously served as the Minister of Rural Development and Panchayati Raj from May 2009 to January 2011.

Dr. Joshi has served as Member of the Rajasthan Legislative Assembly for four terms (1980-2008) where he served in several ministerial capacities as

Minister of Panchayati Raj, Education, Rural Development, Public Health Policy and Planning and Information Technology in the Government of Rajasthan. He has also been the President of Rajasthan Pradesh Congress Committee. Dr. Joshi is the President of Rajasthan Cricket Association.

Connie Rahakundini Bakrie

Ms. Connie Rahakundini Bakrie is an Executive Director of Institute of Defence and Security Studies (IODAS). She is on the Board of Trustee of Indonesian Maritime Institute (IMI) and the Centre of Foreign Affairs and Security Studies (CEFAS).

Ms. Connie Rahakundini Bakrie is a defence analyst and a writer of two important books about Indonesian Military and Defence. She is a lecturer at Faculty of Social and Political Science at the University of Indonesia and a visiting lecturer at the Navy Command Collage and Susjemen Kemenhan. During the past 3 years she has delivered important speeches about Indonesian military, among others in at the National Defence University (NDU) and The East West Center, Washington D.C.

Ms. Connie Rahakundini Bakrie is President of IWAPSI Women Association, one of the biggest women association in Indonesia with a member spread throughout 27 provinces in Indonesia.

Seri S. Samy Vellu

Datuk Seri S. Samy Vellu is the Government of Malaysia's Special Envoy to India and South Asia on Infrastructure. He has served in the government in different capacities as Minister of Works, Minister of Energy, Telecommunications and Posts and Deputy Minister of Local Government and Housing.

In his political career he remained the President of Malaysian Indian Congress, a partner in the ruling National Front Coalition until his retirement in December 2010. He was elected on several occasions as member of the House of Representatives of Malaysian Parliament.

Dato' Samy Vellu is the recipient of innumerable awards including the

Pravasi Bharatiya Samman awarded by the Indian Government. He has helped to set up several educational institutions across the country and worked for the welfare of the working class.

William R. Stevenson

Major General Dato' Dr. William R. Stevenson is a serving military officer in the Malaysian Armed Forces. Currently, he is holding the appointment of Executive Director of Malaysian Institute of Defence and Security (MIDAS), a think tank established under the Ministry of Defence. He is also holding the appointment of Inspector-General of the Malaysian Armed Forces.

Maj Gen Stevenson earned a Master of Business Administration (MBA) degree from Herriot Watt University, Edinburgh, UK and graduated with a Doctorate in Philosophy majoring in Training Management from University Putra Malaysia.

Dipankar Banerjee

Major General Dr. Dipankar Banerjee served in the Indian Army for thirty-six years before pursuing a full-time career in strategic affairs. For the last two decades he has held senior director level positions at leading think tanks in India and the region. For the last seven years he heads the new Delhi-based Institute of Peace and Conflict Studies (IPCS), which is currently ranked among the leading think tanks in Asia.

Major General Banerjee was a member of the International Advisory Group of the ICRC, Geneva, and a consultant to the UN Group of Government Experts on Conventional Arms. He led the campaign for global elimination of land mines and addressed the plenary session at the Treaty signing conference at Ottawa in December 1997. He was involved with the UN Secretary-General's High Level Panel in 2004 as an international advisor in Asia. In this capacity he participated in major international consultations at Singapore, Hangzhou, Kyoto and others. He convened and organized the South Asian Consultation of the High Level Panel at Delhi.

Gopa Sabharwal

Dr Gopa Sabharwal is Vice-Chancellor (Designate) of Nalanda University. Prior to joining the Nalanda University, Dr. Sabharwal taught Sociology at the Lady Shri Ram College for Women, New Delhi, one of the premier women's Colleges in the country. She set up this department in 1993 and has also been its longest serving Chair.

Dr. Sabharwal has written extensively on various aspects of ethnicity and Indian ethnic groups especially in the southern Indian state of Karnataka. Her research in this area led to the publication of the book entitled *Ethnicity and Class: Social Divisions in an Indian City* (2006).

Dr. Sabharwal's another book titled *India since 1947: The Independent Years* (2007), is a detailed time line of events over sixty years of Indian Independence. Dr. Sabharwal is also author of another important book titled *The Indian Millennium - A.D. 1000 to A.D. 2000* (2000) that provides a social history of thousand years and reads like a chronicle of India.

Hidetoshi Nishimura

Mr. Hidetoshi Nishimura is the founding Executive Director of Economic Research Institute for ASEAN and East Asia (ERIA) since June 2008. Mr Nishimura has served for nearly 30 years in the Ministry of International Trade and Industry (MITI which is now known as METI), Japan. He has held important positions in the Policy Division pertaining to environment protection, territorial trade policy on Europe, Africa and Middle East. He was also the Asia Pacific Representative of Japan Overseas Development Corporation (JODC, Bangkok) during which time he conducted Asia-Japan cooperation under various schemes.

His other achievements lie in the compilation of Bogor Declaration of Asia-Pacific Economic Cooperation (APEC). Mr Nishimura has single handedly contributed to Japan-China economic relations during his tenure as the Executive Managing Director of Japan-China Economic Association. During this time, he had the distinction of steering the policy information on China.

Mr Nishimura is alumnus of University of Tokyo where he did a Major in Law for his Bachelor Degree. He obtained his Masters Degree from Yale University.

K. Kesavapany

Ambassador K. Kesavapany began his term as Director of the Institute of Southeast Asian Studies (ISEAS), Singapore, from November 2002. Prior to his appointment to ISEAS, Ambassador Kesavapany was Singapore's High Commissioner to Malaysia from March 1997. In his thirty-year career in the Foreign Service, he served as Permanent Representative to the United Nations in Geneva (December 1991-March 1997) and held key staff appointments in the Ministry of Foreign Affairs, including Director of ASEAN, Director of Directorate II (North America and Europe) and Director of Directorate IV (International Organization and Third World).

Ambassador Kesavapany was an active participant in the final phase of the Uuguay Round negotiations. He was unanimously chosen as the first Chairman of the WTO's General Council in 1995. Subsequently, he played a key role in securing Singapore as the venue for the first WTO Ministerial Meeting in 1996.

K.S. Nathan

Professor K.S. Nathan is the Director of the Institute of Malaysian & International Studies (IKMAS), National University of Malaysia was born and educated in Kuala Lumpur, Malaysia. Professor Nathan has served as a Senior Fellow at the Institute of Southeast Asian Studies (ISEAS) in Singapore from 2001 until March 2007. Currently he is Deputy Director of the Institute of Occidental Studies (IKON), and also Head of the Centre for American Studies (KAMERA, w.e.f. 1 April 2007) in IKON, Universiti Kebangsaan Malaysia, Bangi.

Prof. Nathan has also served as the first President of the Malaysian International Affairs Forum (MIAF), and the Malaysian Association for

American Studies (MAAS), both of which were founded in 1983. He is also the current President of the Malaysian Association for American Studies (MAAS), and has served on the Editorial Board of the *Australian Journal of International Affairs*. He was the Editor of the ISEAS journal *Contemporary Southeast Asia* from January 2003 to April 2007. Professor Nathan has served as a Consultant to several Institutions of Higher Learning and Research in Malaysia and Singapore.

Kasit Piromya

H.E. Mr. Kasit Piromya is the Minister of Foreign Affairs, Royal Kingdom of Thailand. He has served in the Ministry of Foreign Affairs for thirty-seven years. During those years he served as the Director of Policy and Planning Division, Deputy Director-General in the Economic Affairs Department, and Ambassador to Moscow, Jakarta, Bonn/Berlin, Tokyo and Washington D.C.

H.E. Piromya has been a member of the Democrat Party of Thailand, Advisor to the Party leadership, a member of the Shadow Cabinet (2008), and the Chairman of the Committee on the Promotion of Democracy within the Party. He holds diploma in international relations from the Institute of Social Sciences, the Hague, The Netherlands.

Kavi Chongkittavorn

Mr. Kavi Chongkittavorn is a regular contributor on regional affairs to *The Nation*, a major English language daily in Thailand published from Bangkok. He has also been its Editor. He has been writing for the past three decades on domestic and regional politics.

Mr. Chongkittavorn was Bureau Chief in Phnom Penh from 1987-88 and in Hanoi from 1989-91. Currently, he is also the host of "Inside Asia", a current affair television programme.

Mahanai Zainal Abidin

Dato' Dr. Mahani Zainal Abidin was appointed Chief Executive of the Institute of Strategic and International Studies (ISIS) Malaysia in January 2010 and prior to that she was the Director-General of the Institute from May 2007 to December 2009. She served as Deputy Chairman of the National Accreditation Board from May 2003 until October 2007. In 1998, Dr. Mahani was appointed a Member of the Working Group for the National Economic Action Council, a body established by the Malaysian Government to formulate measures to initiate recovery from the financial crisis.

Dr. Mahani's research interests are in industrial policy, international trade and regional integration and economic structural transformation. Her book on *The Malaysian Crisis Management Model: Rewriting the Rules* was published in 2002.

Dato' Dr. Mahani Zainal Abidin is a Council Member of the National Economic Advisory Council (NEAC), established in July 2009 to advise the Government on a new national economic model for Malaysia. She is also a Trustee of Yayasan Malaysia; a Commission Member of the Land Public Transport Commission; and a Member of International Steering Committee for the Pacific Trade and Development (PAFTAD).

Mari Elka Pangestu

H.E. Dr. Mari Elka Pangestu is currently the Minister of Trade and is the only Cabinet Member of ethnic Chinese descent. Prior to becoming the Minister of Trade, she was an instructor in the Faculty of Economics in the University of Indonesia. She was active for a long time in the Trade Forum (TF) as the Programme Coordinator of the Pacific Economic Cooperation Council (PECC), a private networking organization comprising of 23 member economies in the Asia Pacific region.

Dr. Mari Pangestu has been one of the foremost economics experts in Indonesia. She serves on the Board of External Editors of the *Asian Journal of Business* (University of Michigan) and *Bulletin of Indonesian Economic Studies* (Australian National University). She is also the co-coordinator of the Task Force on Poverty and Development for the United Nations Millennium Project.

As a noted economist, Dr. Pangestu has earned acknowledgement from the World Bank, the International Monetary Fund and the Asian Development Bank. She has published widely in the Indonesian and international media.

Maria Ligia Noronha

Dr. Maria Ligia Noronha is a Senior Fellow at The Energy and Resources Institute (TERI), India, and Director of its Resources, Regulation and Global Security Division. She is Secretary of the Asian Energy Institute, a network of Asian and non-Asian institutes, was Coordinator of Renewable Energy and Energy Efficiency Partnership (REEEP), South Asia during 2005-09, and is the Michael Hintze Energy Security Visiting Senior Fellow at the Centre for International Security Studies (CISS), University of Sydney, Australia, 2009-11.

She has served on several expert panels of the Government of India including the Expert Committee on Climate Change (2007-10), Western Ghats Ecology Expert Panel, and the Task Force on Natural Resources, Commission on Centre State Relations. She is currently a member of the Planning Board, Government of Goa and on Goa's Jubilee Development Council. She is also a member of the Global Agenda Council on Mines and Metals of the World Economic Forum. Dr. Noronha has a Masters in Economics from the University of Bombay, a Masters in Sea Use Law, Economics, and Policy, and a Ph.D. from the London School of Economics.

Mushahid Ali

Ambassador Mushahid Ali is Senior Fellow at the S. Rajaratnam School of International Studies, and a diplomatic veteran. He was a member of the Singapore Foreign Service for over thirty-one years (1970-2001), and has served in various overseas missions including Kuala Lumpur, Tokyo, London, Jakarta, Hong Kong and Riyadh. He was Chief of Protocol from 1991 to 1995 and served as Ambassador to Cambodia from 1995 to 2000.

On retirement from the Foreign Service he joined the Institute of Defence and Strategic Studies, the forerunner of RSIS, where he was Senior Fellow until late 2004. He has attended many international and regional conferences of ASEAN, the Commonwealth and United Nations, as well as regional academic and research institutions. Ambassador Ali was conferred the Public Administration Medal (Silver) by the President of Singapore and Commander, Royal Order of Sahametrei by the King of Cambodia.

Ong Keng Yong

Ambassador Ong Keng Yong is Director of the Institute of Policy Studies in the Lee Kuan Yew School of Public Policy at the National University of Singapore. He is concurrently Ambassador-at-Large in the Singapore Ministry of Foreign Affairs and Singapore's Non-resident Ambassador to Iran. He was ASEAN Secretary-General from January 2003 to January 2008 and Singapore's Ambassador to India and Nepal from 1996-98. He is a graduate of the University of Singapore and Georgetown University, Washington DC, USA.

Pehin Dato Lim Jock Seng

H.E. Pehin Dato Lim Jock Seng is the Minister of Foreign Affairs and Trade II, Government of Brunei Darussalam. He has held several important positions in the government including Second Minister of Foreign Affairs, Chairman of the Board of Directors of Royal Brunei Airlines, Chairman of Brunei Shell Petroleum Company, Member of the Legislative Council and Member of the Privy Council.

H.E. Pehin Dato Seng has also served in several other official capacities in the Ministry of Foreign Affairs as Permanent Secretary, Director of Politics and also Brunei's High Commissioner to New Zealand. He has received several awards, titles and decorations.

H.E. Pehin Dato Seng has received Honorary Fellowship from the University College of Swansea and Royal Anthropological Institute, London

Pham Quang Vinh

H.E. Mr. Pham Quang Vinh is currently the Assistant Minister for Foreign Affairs, and the ASEAN SOM (Senior Officials' Meeting) leader. He served as the Deputy Director-General and Director-General in the Ministry of Foreign Affairs.

H.E. Mr. Pham Quang Vinh has served in several diplomatic missions abroad including Permanent Mission of Vietnam to the United Nations, New York and Vietnam's embassy in Bangkok. He also served in different capacities in several departments of the Ministry of Foreign Affairs, Vietnam.

H.E. Mr. Pham Quang Vinh graduated from the University of Foreign Affairs, Hanoi and has a postgraduation degree from Canberra College of Advanced Education, Australia.

R. Ravindran

Mr Ravindran is currently the Chairman of SAEA Group Research Pvt. Ltd., Singapore. He is a Consultant with INCA LAW LLC in Singapore. He also sits as a Director on the board of SGX listed companies and several private companies.

He was a Member of Parliament in Singapore for the Marine Parade Group Representation Constituency and the Bukit Timah Group Representation Constituency from 1997 to 2006.

His other prior appointments include Chairman of the Government Parliamentary Committee for Defence and Foreign Affairs, Board Member of the People's Association, and Deputy Chairman in the Government Parliamentary Committee for Home Affairs and Law, and a member of the Jurong Town Council and Marine Parade Town Council, the South East Community Development Council, the Singapore Institute of Directors and the Singapore Academy of Law.

Rodolfo C. Severino

Mr. Rodolfo Severino is a former Secretary-General of ASEAN from 1998 to 2002 and currently the head of the ASEAN Studies Centre at the Institute of Southeast Asian Studies in Singapore. Before serving as ASEAN Secretary-General, Mr Severino was Under Secretary of Foreign Affairs of the Philippines.

In the Philippine Foreign Service, Mr Severino had postings in Malaysia, Beijing and Washington, D.C.

He has authored several books including *Southeast Asia in Search of an ASEAN Community*. He has also published several other works on ASEAN, including a volume on the ASEAN Regional Forum. He has recently published a book on the Philippines' national territory.

S.M. Krishna

Shri S.M. Krishna is the External Affairs Minister, Government of India. Mr. Krishna made his debut in Parliament in 1968 to become a Member of the fourth Lok Sabha. He returned to the provincial politics of Karnataka in 1972 and was inducted as Minister for Commerce, Industries and Parliamentary Affairs.

Shri Krishna returned to the Lok Sabha in 1980 and served in different capacities as Minister of State for Industry and Minister of State for Finance till 1985. He was elected to Rajya Sabha in 1996, and was a member till October 1999.

He was elected as the Chief Minister of Karnataka in October 1999 and served till may 2004. Mr. Krishna assumed office of Governor of Maharashtra in December 2004 and remained in the post till March 2008. He was re-elected as member of the Rajya Sabha on 19 June 2008.

Widely travelled, Shri Krishna was a member of the Indian delegation to the UN in 1982, and a delegate to the Commonwealth Parliamentary Seminar at Westminister, UK in 1990.

Sabam P. Siagian

Mr. Siagian is the Director and Senior Editor of the *Jakarta Post*. He is a Board member of the *Jakarta Post* publishing company and a consultant with several international companies. He was appointed as a member of the People's Consultative Assembly (MPR) from 1999 to 2004.

Mr. Siagian worked as President of Indonesia-Australia Business Council from 1996 to 2000 and served on the Panel of Tangguh Independent Advisory Panel (TIAP) to BP's LNG Project in Papua, 2002-09. Mr. Siagian also served as Ambassador for Indonesia to Australia from 1991 to 1995.

He was a Nieman Fellow, Journalism, Harvard University, Cambridge, Massachusetts, USA and later on worked as Visiting Fellow in the Center for International Affairs, Georgetown University, Washington, DC.

Samuel Blancaflor Bagasin

Mr. Samuel Blancaflor Bagasin is presently the Under-Secretary for Civil, Veterans and Reserve Affairs at the Philippine Department of National Defense (DND). He assists the Secretary of National Defense in overseeing the Office of Civil Defense (OCD) and the Philippine Veterans Affairs Office (PVAO).

Mr. Bagasin retired in 2006 with the rank of Lieutenant General in the Armed Forces of the Philippines (AFP) after thirty-eight years of military service. He served in various capacities as Company Commander, Battalion Commander and other staff positions both in the Philippine Army and at the Headquarters of the Armed Forces of the Philippines.

Under-Secretary Bagasin obtained a Masters Degree in National Security Administration at the National Defense College of the Philippines in 1995 and Masters Degree in Business at Webster University, Missouri, USA in 1993.

Shivshankar Menon

Shri Shivshankar Menon is National Security Advisor to the Prime Minister of India since January 2010. Shri Menon was previously Foreign Secretary of India from October 2006 to August 2009. He has served as Ambassador and High Commissioner of India to Israel (1995-97), Sri Lanka (1997-2000), China (2000-03) and Pakistan (2003-06). He was also a member of the Atomic Energy Commission in 2008-09.

A career diplomat, Shri Menon served in China (thrice), in Japan, and in Austria in the Embassy and the mission to the IAEA and UN. He was seconded to the Department of Atomic Energy in the early 1980s. His professional experience included India's relations with her neighbours, atomic energy and disarmament issues, and India's relations with the major powers. Shri Menon speaks Chinese and German.

Sudhir T. Devare

Shri Devare is the Director-General, Indian Council of World Affairs, New Delhi, one of the oldest think tanks in India. He served for thirty-seven years in the Indian Foreign Service before retiring as a Secretary in the Ministry of External Affairs, Government of India. He has also been closely associated with the formulation of India's Look East policy.

Shri Devare was India's Ambassador to South Korea, Ukraine, Armenia, Georgia and Indonesia. He also led the Indian official level delegation in several international forums such as the ASEAN Regional Forum, Group of 77, IOR-ARC, BIMSTEC, etc.

Shri Devare has been a member of the National Security Advisory Board, Government of India, member of CSCAP-India, and member of Eminent Persons' and Experts' Group of the ARF. He was Vice-Chairman of the Research & Information System (RIS) for Developing Countries, New Delhi. He worked as a Visiting Professor at the Jawaharlal Nehru University, New Delhi, Visiting Senior Research Fellow at the Institute of Southeast Asian Studies, Singapore and a Fellow at the Weatherhead Center for International Affairs, Harvard University. He has authored and edited books on India and Southeast Asia, and has written on various aspects of Indian diplomacy and regional affairs in the Asia-Pacific.

Surin Pitsuwan

H.E. Dr. Surin Pitsuwan is the Secretary-General of ASEAN. He served as Chair of the ASEAN Ministerial Meeting and the Chair of the ASEAN Regional Forum (ARF) in 1999-2000.

During his political career, Dr. Pitsuwan served as Minister of Foreign Affairs from 1997 to 2001, the Deputy Minister for Foreign Affairs during 1992-95, Secretary to Deputy Minister of Interior, and Secretary to the Speaker of the House of Representatives (Chuan Leekpai). Dr. Pitsuwan was a Deputy Leader of the Democrat Party, Thailand.

Upon leaving the foreign affairs portfolio in mid-2001, Dr. Surin was appointed a member of the Commission on Human Security of the United Nations until 2003. He is currently on the Advisory Board of the UN Human Security Trust Fund; the Advisory Board of the International Crisis Group (ICG); a member of the International Advisory Board of the Council on Foreign Relations in New York; and an International Academic Advisor of the Centre for Islamic Studies, Oxford University.

Dr. Pitsuwan taught at the Faculty of Political Science at Thammasat University from 1978-83 and 1984-86.

Tan Tai Yong

Prof. Tan Tai Yong is the Director of Institute of South Asian Studies, Singapore. He was previously the Dean of Faculty of Social Sciences; Head of the Department of History; and also Acting Director of the Institute of South Asian Studies in the National University of Singapore.

Prof. Yong has been a visiting faculty member in the Cambridge University and University of London. Prof. Yong has published extensively on different aspects of India and South Asia. Prof. Yong is on the editorial board of several academic journals of international repute. Besides, Prof. Yong has been a member of various management boards, boards of trustees, governmental panels and committees.

U Nyunt Maung Shein

H.E. Mr. U Nyunt Maung Shein has served the government of Myanmar for forty years before retiring as Representative to the United Nations Office, Geneva in 2008. H.E. Mr. U Nyunt Maung Shein served in various capacities at Myanmar Missions in Bern, Hanoi, Bangkok, Dhaka and Tokyo. He was Ambassador Extraordinary and Plenipotentiary to the Republic of Korea (2001-02) and the Federal Republic of Germany (2002-05) with concurrent accreditation to Austria, Poland, Finland and the Czech Republic, as well as Permanent Representative to the UNIDO, UNODC and IAEA, Vienna.

H.E. Mr. U Nyunt Maung Shein served in the Political Department, Ministry of Foreign Affairs in different capacities as Director of Boundary Division (1990-92), Deputy Director-General (1996) and Director-General (1998-2000). He has represented his country at the Senior Officials' Meeting (SOM) and other related meetings of ASEAN including summits.